Her Work

Live LOVE Lead

A Woman's Guide to Living on Purpose

TANNA ABRAHAM

This book is dedicated to LaTasha, Yonique, Mallory, Portia, Shanelle, Wendy, China, Alani, and all the incredible women I've had the privilege of journeying with over the years through small groups, book clubs, workshops, and preaching. Thank you for consistently showing up, engaging in transformative discussions, and for the unwavering faith you've placed in me and my leadership.

Contents

Introduction

Hey lady,

I'm thrilled that you've chosen to explore this book. It has resided in my heart for a few years, undergoing numerous iterations in my mind. This moment feels like the perfect time for me to write it, and I'm confident that it's the right time for you to read it.

I hit the big 4-0 a few months ago, and let me tell you, the first day of forty was a tough pill to swallow. There was no celebrating. In fact, my son was sick with strep throat, and I wasn't feeling my best, both physically and emotionally. To top it off, I severed three friendships that day. My birthday was on a Monday, and all week I kept thinking, "Is this what forty is all about? Hurt, pain, disappointment, and inconvenience?"

In the following days, I gained clarity, perspective, acceptance, and eventually peace. I came to realize what many have said about getting older: With age comes wisdom, boldness, low tolerance, and a deep appreciation for life. You move from realizing, to accepting that life is fickle, imperfect, unpredictable, and precious. The reality that you only have one life to live becomes palpable, and for some, it sobers you from wasting time on the mundane and trivial things, teaching you how to embrace life's journey with all that comes with it.

I recently came across a social media post suggesting that if you're between thirty-six and forty-five, this is considered your midlife, given the current life expectancy. Midlife?! Initially, I found it amusing. Then, I had one of those moments where I paused and screamed on the inside. After that, all I could think about was how I am living. I even considered what my definition of living looks like, and honestly, I struggled to define it. Outside of life's regular happenings and the things that make me happy, I couldn't arrive at a suitable definition for myself; I just knew that the way I'm currently living is not it.

I've come to realize that I'm not alone with these sentiments, as many women have recently opened up to me about their discontent with life and the challenges they face in figuring out how to make meaningful changes. Moreover, they feel guilt when expressing it out loud because they fear judgment from others, or worse, they are secretly judging themselves. Yet, it's a reality we all must face.

Yes, I've been alive for forty years but I can't say with certainty that I've been living for forty years. I've experienced a lot of loss in the past two years and it really caused me to consider my own mortality and evaluate the way I'm choosing to live. I say *choosing* because we all have a choice in how we live our lives. We can blame others for our present circumstances but the truth is, we have the power to create the life we want. I believe, that some of us have trouble figuring out how to exercise our inner power and how to use that power to fuel a purpose-filled life.

The inspiration behind my writing of *Her Work* stems from a deep understanding that genuine fulfillment cannot be confined to a single word or definition. It necessitates a holistic perspective, considering all aspects of our lives and womanhood. By recognizing both the joys and lessons, we can start to envision the potential for fully living a purposeful life. My prayer is that this book will serve as a guide to get you there.

So let's get started.

With love,

Tanna

CHAPTER 1

The Journey

When I was in the ninth grade, I participated in the Miss FHA (Future Homemakers of America) pageant. Yes, it was a club at my school, and yes, I was a member. My friends chuckled when I told them about my membership because it's hard to imagine such a club in 2024. Later in my high school years, the name was changed from FHA to FCCLA (Family, Career and Community Leaders of America), which it currently exists as. I came from a very pageant-centric island where there was a pageant opportunity for everything, so a Miss FHA pageant was not unusual.

Recalling my introductory speech for the pageant, which I wrote, I opened with a quote that I heard earlier that year: "Success is a journey, not a destination, and half the fun is getting there."

At the age of fourteen, I didn't grasp the full significance of that quote; all I knew was that it caught my attention when I first heard it and continues to resonate with me today.

As a girl with hopes, dreams, and some grandiose illusions of what my life would look like as I grew up, I turned to this quote for hope and grounding in moments when life didn't unfold as I had imagined. The vision of the white picket fence, two dogs, and six kids (yes, six!), a thriving career, and of course, a husband resembling Morris Chestnut with the voice of Idris Elba and a smile like LL Cool J was all part of my dream. However, as I reached thirty, reality hit: I was a struggling single parent with no potential partner in sight. Despite finding success in various ways, not meeting the expectations I had set for myself left me dealing with loneliness, disappointment, and questions. Moreover, in this social media-saturated era where we have a picture-perfect view of everyone's dreams coming true, or at least that's the way it's perceived, it's hard not to look at yourself and ask the question, "Is it just me?" It's hard to find the fun in the journey when the destination seems so far off.

I'm sure you have experienced the disappointment of not reaching certain milestones you set for yourself throughout your life. Even after reciting the quotes and affirmations, creating countless vision boards, and repeating the same prayer, you still find yourself not where you expected to be at this point in your life. Sis, if no one has said it to you yet, let me be the first to say, "It's OK." The very fact that you are reading this right now means you're still breathing. AND, if you're still breathing then it means you are still on the journey.

It's easy to forget that, unlike an airplane whose focus is on the next destination, life is all about the journey. What we often perceive as destinations are merely stops resulting from the choices we've made along the journey. The true destination reveals itself at the end of life.

Choices

One of the poems that has held a special place in my heart since I first read it is "The Road Not Taken" by Robert Frost.

> Two roads diverged in a yellow wood,
> And sorry I could not travel both
> And be one traveler, long I stood
> And looked down one as far as I could
> To where it bent in the undergrowth;
> Then took the other, as just as fair,
> And having perhaps the better claim,
> Because it was grassy and wanted wear;
> Though as for that the passing there
> Had worn them really about the same,
> And both that morning equally lay
> In leaves no step had trodden black.
> Oh, I kept the first for another day!

Yet knowing how way leads on to way,
I doubted if I should ever come back.
I shall be telling this with a sigh
Somewhere ages and ages hence:
Two roads diverged in a wood, and I—
I took the one less traveled by,
And that has made all the difference.

This poem beautifully explores the choices we face in life and the conflicts within us when we reflect on what might have been. As 2023 came to a close, I started thinking about my choices over the years. There's something about the turn of the decade, milestone birthdays and the start of a new year that sparks introspection and perspective. In those last few days before the new year, I wondered about what could have been—what if I did things differently, why I didn't, and what if I chose another path? Usually, when I have times of reflection I would reassure myself that the way I'm going is the right way. I would spiritualize it and say, "I am right where God wants me to be" or "All things work together for good." However, this time, I let myself consider all the other possibilities. What if I went to that school? What if I didn't move to that state? What if I didn't fumble that opportunity? What if I entered into that relationship? What if I asked for help when I needed it? What if I took the risk? Where would I be now? How different would my life be? Would my struggles be the same, or would things have been a lot easier?

I replayed this over in my mind for days, reliving many decisions between age twenty and age forty. I thought about every possible way my life could have gone. I analyzed every poor choice, bad decision, obstacle, success and even the joys and sadness along the way. Even without a Juris Doctorate, I argued both sides of my choices and questions before the juror of my thoughts. In the end, it was a hung jury. I didn't arrive at any clear conclusions. The only thing I was sure of, was that I can't relive the past, I can only commit to learning from the past and intentionally living in the present.

It's so easy to get entangled in past mistakes, wrong turns, and questionable choices. Many live in the present, wishing they could rewrite the past. Or worst, they remain fixated on the past, hoping that it will rewrite the present. We've all encountered individuals who can't let a conversation pass without reminiscing about their high school or college days, or what they were like in their twenties. I know someone who consistently says, "I used to be successful," dedicating more time to reflecting on past achievements than striving to enhance their present or future. While reflection is valuable, it shouldn't transform into dwelling, as dwelling suggests living or residing in that particular thought. It's crucial to strike a healthy balance.

We cannot travel back in time and explore different choices, as I once saw in a Hallmark Christmas movie. What truly matters are the choices we make in the present and the impact they will have on our future.

We are on a journey, and on that journey we will encounter highs and lows, joys and sorrows, disappointment and gratitude, missed opportunities and great successes. And yes, we will reflect along the way but let's commit to reflect and not dwell. Let's commit to spending our time thinking and praying about the choices ahead, the road we are presently traveling. Let's commit to making decisions, sometimes with certainty, other times by faith, that help to shape our future. Let's commit to enjoying the journey; after all, it's the journey of a lifetime, literally.

Pause, Consider, Take Action

1. What have you been focusing your thoughts on lately?

2. Reflect on how your current thought patterns are influencing your present circumstances. How do these thoughts shape your actions and decisions in your day-to-day life?

3. Decide what you need to shift, first in your thoughts and ultimately in your life, to align with the future that God has envisioned for you. Reflect on specific areas where this shift may be necessary. What are some practical steps you can take to initiate this transformation?

CHAPTER 2

Navigating the Path Forward

I know what you're thinking: "That last chapter was beautifully written (at least that's what I was thinking), and I resonated with it on so many levels, but how do I proceed? How do I move forward after confronting regrets and missed opportunities?"

First, I want to acknowledge that I don't have all the answers. This book serves as a guide, offering tools to help you navigate your own path forward. However, to better assist you, I am pleased to introduce three women in the Bible navigating their own tumultuous journeys. Ruth chapter 1 is a captivating narrative that delves into the themes of loss, devotion, choices and resilience amid adversity. While this story might be familiar to you, I urge you to set aside any preconceived notions and approach it with fresh eyes.

It all started when a severe famine struck their homeland. Elimelech, a man from Bethlehem in Judah, along with his wife, Naomi, and sons, Mahlon and Kilion, faced the harsh realities of life in the midst of scarcity. To secure a future, they left their homeland and settled in the foreign land of Moab.

Moab marked a fresh start for Elimelech's family, but tragedy quickly followed. After Elimelech's death, Naomi found herself a widow, while her sons married Moabite women, Orpah and Ruth. Over the span of a decade, both sons also passed away, leaving Naomi and her daughters-in-law to grapple with grief upon grief.

Can you picture it? Each time Naomi tries to regain her footing, another life-altering event occurs. It's one thing to lose a husband, but she also loses both sons. The pain, the emptiness, the deepening sorrow Naomi must have felt is unimaginable. What now? What's the next step? How does she move forward? Perhaps at some point in your life, you've experienced a similar situation, where life's storms seem relentless, knocking you off balance again and again. That's the place Naomi was in, and I imagine Ruth and Orpah weren't far off.

News reached Naomi in Moab that the Lord had blessed Judah with abundance. Stirred by this new hope, she decided to return to her homeland, urging her daughters-in-law to stay in Moab. Tearful goodbyes ensued, and while Orpah chose to remain, Ruth clung steadfastly to Naomi. Despite Naomi's attempts to dissuade her, Ruth insisted on accompanying her back to Judah. With heart-stirring words often repeated in wedding vows and other committal ceremonies, Ruth pledged allegiance to Naomi, promising to share her fate and adopt her people and God as her own.

The journey back to Bethlehem was filled with emotion. As they arrived, the townspeople were abuzz with excitement, wondering if the woman returning was indeed Naomi. Reflecting the bitterness that life had dealt her, Naomi chose to be called Mara.

All three women found themselves on the brink of a new chapter in their individual journeys. While the fate of Orpah remains a mystery beyond her return to her family, the focus of the book, titled Ruth, initially centers around Naomi's journey. However, as we progress into chapters 2–4, the spotlight shifts to Ruth. Throughout these chapters, I've gleaned three invaluable lessons that have profoundly influenced my own journey, and I hope they will be of benefit to you.

1. Acknowledge Where You've Been

Acknowledging your past is the initial step toward healing and progress. Although you don't need to broadcast it to everyone, being honest with yourself, with God and sometimes with a trusted friend or therapist is crucial.

Arriving back in Bethlehem, Naomi encountered old friends and didn't attempt to mask her pain. Instead, she openly acknowledged the bitter reality of her situation. She rejected her former name, Naomi, and chose to be called Mara, signifying the bitterness that had consumed her. Naomi's honesty is a powerful lesson—she didn't hide behind a facade but confronted her anguish head-on. It's a reminder that it's OK to acknowledge your struggles instead of pretending everything is fine. And yes, you can do that without changing your name.

Like Naomi, you might have encountered similar trials, navigating various forms of loss—physical, emotional, and social. You might grapple with grief, depression, and anxiety, struggling to maintain your faith and find hope amid uncertainty. I have personally experienced the reluctance to confront emotions. There are moments when you convince yourself that it's simpler to deny what happened or convince yourself that you're moving forward, rather than pausing to acknowledge the pain, hurt, and discomfort. You might even mask your pain behind social media personas and unhealthy habits and behaviors, portraying a life of bliss while internally grappling with turmoil.

It's essential to pause and confront the facades you may be upholding. These facades could be the very barriers that are preventing you from progressing and finding a way forward. Allowing yourself to acknowledge where you've been and experience the necessary emotions is crucial to embarking on a journey of healing. This entails facing your emotions, which can be painful at times. It also involves understanding the depth of our experiences and giving ourselves the opportunity to mourn, heal, and ultimately, evolve. By taking the time to engage in genuine introspection and soul-searching, I assure you that there will come a time when you can reflect on those challenging seasons with a smile. You may even find yourself laughing when you contemplate how far you've come from where you once were. I often say to myself, "If only my younger self were to see me now, it wouldn't even recognize me." Only by acknowledging your past can you truly embrace the journey ahead.

The next time we are made aware that Naomi encounters the townspeople is in chapter 4. "Praise be to the Lord," they proclaimed, "who has not left you without a guardian-redeemer." They spoke of a future filled with blessings and renewal, assuring Naomi that she would not be abandoned in her old age. As Naomi held the child born to Ruth, she embraced the promise of a new beginning. The women of the village rejoiced at the sight, declaring, "Naomi has a son!"

The story comes full circle. Again they referred to her as Naomi, but this time she does not object. Acknowledging where you've been is not the end; rather, it points you in the direction of a new beginning.

2. Don't Compare Your Journey

If I could highlight, bold, underline, and enlarge this point without it being excessive, I would. This lesson is one of the holy grail of all life's lessons. So much of the disappointment and frustration we experience on the journey comes from comparing ourselves to others. Some might say, "I'm just referencing their life as a gauge to ensure that I'm on the right path" or "I'm just looking at them for inspiration." And though it seems there's no harm in that, let me caution you that there is a thin line between comparison and reference and that line can be easily crossed.

Over the past month, I've really come to enjoy using the rowing machines at the gym and have made them a regular part of my routine. I started with just a few minutes at light resistance and gradually worked my way up. Now, I'm comfortably rowing for twenty minutes at a moderate resistance.

The other day, while I was rowing, I noticed two people hop onto the machines near mine. They immediately started rowing at a very fast pace, and here I was, focused on pacing myself to get through my twenty minutes. Seeing them row so fast made me feel a bit self-conscious, and I started pushing myself harder, trying to keep up with their speed. But I quickly realized that I wouldn't be able to sustain that pace and returned to my usual speed.

To my surprise, those two folks ended their workout in less than five minutes, well before their planned time. It made me realize that if I had tried to match their speed, I might have ended up quitting as well. This experience was a great reminder that it's important to focus on my own progress rather than comparing myself to others. Everyone's journey is different, and it's best to stick to your own path. You can wave to others along the way but don't waver; stay true to your own pace and path. Which is what I believe Orpah did.

Ultimately, Naomi decides to return to Bethlehem upon hearing of the Lord's provisions there. She advises her daughters-in-law to return to their homes and prays for the Lord's blessing upon them. Orpah chooses to return home after Naomi declares she has nothing left to offer them. On the other hand, Ruth insists on staying with Naomi. While we only learn about Ruth's journey after she follows Naomi, it's important to recognize that neither path was inherently better, as they were both integral parts of their respective journeys.

Many have unfairly criticized Orpah for her decision not to accompany Naomi and Ruth, assuming the worst because we are not informed of her fate. If there were a book detailing Orpah's life and revealing that she experienced a similar outcome to Ruth's, we would likely view her as being in God's will and on the right path. However, the uncertainty surrounding Orpah's story fills us with anxiety—fear of the unknown, and instead of acknowledging our lack of information, we tend to cast a shadow over her journey.

Let's be honest: Many of us have been guilty of allowing uncertainty to hold us back. When we don't have or see a clear plan for our own story, we hesitate to move forward and end up trying to follow someone else's path just because we can see where it took them. Instead of taking a leap of faith and trusting in God to lead us on our own unique journey, we're drawn to the idea of following a preset route.

Your journey is uniquely yours, just as Orpah's decision to return home and Ruth's choice to stay with Naomi were right for them. Comparing your journey to someone else's only leads to frustration and missed opportunities that were tailored just for you. Instead of trying to emulate someone else's path, focus on embracing your own journey and the lessons it holds for you. In Jeremiah 29:11, God speaks these words to the people through Jeremiah amid the turmoil of uncertainty and doubt: "For I know the plans I have for you," declares the LORD, "plans to prosper you and not to harm you, plans to give you hope and a future." You don't have to mimic someone else's path; you just need to seek God regarding the plan that was already laid out specifically for you. Follow the plan, embrace the path, and trust that it will lead you where you need to go.

3. Embrace the New

I moved to Houston in the summer of 2023, a decision that was right for the next step of my journey but did not play out the way I had envisioned. When I originally made the decision to move to Houston, I imagined that my life would be a supersized and epic version of what it was, just cheaper;

I would work from home, but from a bigger, much nicer residence. I would find a new worship community and serve on the ministerial staff in a similar capacity as before. My son would attend a larger school, and I would quickly make friends with most of the parents, as I had done previously and I would have a vibrant social life. However, at every turn, I encountered the unexpected. Yes, the cost of living was much more reasonable but the rest did not play out as I anticipated. I tried repeatedly to recreate my previous environment in my new context, attempting to make all the decisions the way I did in the past and trying to cling to some sense of familiarity and comfort. My attempts were all unsuccessful. There was always a barrier preventing me from recreating my past life in Maryland. This frustrated me at first. I was lonely and full of uncertainty. I knew deep down that my decision to move was still right, yet I struggled to embrace what came with the decision: Something New.

As someone who likes to have everything figured out, I struggled with trying to assist God along the way, only causing myself unnecessary grief and disappointment. I eventually recognized the theme of this season of my life as "Something New." I wasn't certain of what that would entail but I knew it was unfamiliar and unlike anything I had experienced before.

Ruth was also in a new city and a new season of her life, but unlike me, she embraced this new place with humility, courage, and diligence. We see in chapter 2 that despite being a foreigner and facing the challenges of widowhood, Ruth exhibited a strong sense of determination and commitment to provide for herself and her mother-in-law. When Naomi suggested that Ruth go to the fields to glean, Ruth willingly embraced the opportunity to work and gather food for their sustenance.

Ruth's willingness to embrace the "new" in her life allowed her to be noticed by Boaz, who later became her husband. Together, they conceived a son named Obed, unaware of the significant role he would play in shaping the history of Israel. Obed would become the father of Jesse, and Jesse would be the father of David, ultimately listing them and Ruth in Matthew chapter 1 as part of the lineage of Jesus.

We often ask and pray for new beginnings in life but truthfully what we're asking for is a revamped version of what we currently have. Think about some of your past relationships, each person was a refurbished version of the previous person. Or think of that "new" job that you prayed for, only to get there and realize the only thing new is the company name and your job title. Without awareness and intentionality, we are prone to linger in familiar territory.

Recently I went to Sweet Frog to get my favorite frozen yogurt flavor that I got all the time in Maryland. I went in ready to fix my fro-yo like I always did and guess what, they didn't have that flavor. At first I thought to myself, you've got to be kidding me. Then I laughed because I realized it was another way I was reaching for the familiar. I walked over to the counter and asked for a few sample cups so I could begin trying out new flavors. I walked out of there with two new flavors, which I very much enjoyed.

One of my favorite pastimes is sifting through my closet to find designer items that I can list for sale on resale sites. What I've noticed when listing the items is that there is a prompt to list the condition of the item. Often, the prompts are followed by an explanation, for example, "Good, with minor scratches." This occurs for every prompt except the "New" prompt. Why? Because "new" simply means new, no other disclaimer is necessary.

"I am about to do a new thing; now it springs forth; do you not perceive it? I will make a way in the wilderness and rivers in the desert." Isaiah 43:19 (NRSV)

God speaks through the prophet Isaiah to the nation of Israel, declaring that He is doing something new and remarkable. He assured them that even in the wilderness, God would make a way, and in the desert, rivers would flow. It was a message of hope and encouragement, reminding the people to trust in God's faithfulness and to look forward to the new things He was bringing about in their midst.

The part of this verse that has been sticking out to me lately is, "Now it springs forth, do you not perceive it?" What this says to me, is that we don't have to keep waiting for the new; it's happening right now but it's up to us to be attentive and discern it and ultimately embrace it by faith. Don't miss the new thing God wants to do in your life because you want to cling to the familiar. Embrace the new!

Pause, Consider, Take Action

1. Answer the questions in the table below.

a. What part of your past have you been hesitant to revisit, and why?

____

____

____

____

b. What specific aspects of that past experience do you need to address in order to facilitate healing and progress?

____

____

c. Who can you reach out to for support in navigating this process effectively? (friend, therapist, pastor, etc.)

2. Is there anyone to whom you've been comparing yourself or your journey? If so, what are some lessons from this chapter that can help you release yourself from that comparison?

3. In what ways do you find yourself resisting change and clinging to the familiar, even when a deeper knowing suggests otherwise?

4. Have you experienced disruptions in your life that, upon reflection, seemed to be guiding you toward something new and transformative?

CHAPTER 3

The Fight of Your Life

I want to begin this chapter by letting you know that you are amazing! You are enough. You are capable. You are worthy. You have what it takes. You are a movement all by yourself. You are a winner. You are unstoppable.

Without even knowing you, I know that these things are true, simply because I know your Creator. I know the quality of your Creator's work. I know your Creator's proven track record and I've seen firsthand the fruits of your Creator's labor. Yet, even with knowledge of the Creator and the Creator's work, many of us struggle to accept the truths of who we are.

I believe that our biggest enemy on this journey of life isn't the devil, your haters, your childhood nemesis, the boss who keeps passing you over for a promotion, that family member who always belittles you, or that person who goes out of their way to prove that they are better than you. No, it's the person staring back at you in the mirror.

Whether you have come to accept it as imposter syndrome, self-doubt, lack of confidence, or fear of failure, the core issue is the same: YOU fighting against you. You, being your own worst enemy and hindering your own progress. For example, you conceive an idea, start working on it, and then suddenly overwhelm yourself with questions for which you don't yet have answers. Which eventually causes you to quit. Or perhaps you're offered a new position, and like any promotion, it requires growth into the role. Yet, you turn down the role or delay your response because you feel unprepared or doubt your abilities. Or, you thoroughly prepare yourself for a new opportunity and when the door opens you tell yourself that this is no longer the right time. Or maybe you meet someone who has the qualities that you've been praying for but you search for everything wrong just to find a reason to bail and say it won't work. I can go on and on with examples of how we get in our own way but I'm sure by now you get the gist and can probably add examples of your own. You can most likely finish up these scenarios for me. Unfortunately, this pattern repeats itself in various aspects of our lives, continuously obstructing our paths forward.

This chapter is not meant to be revelational, but rather to help you accept what you already know, identify the things you don't, and confront them so that you can reduce the delays and unnecessary pit stops on your journey. These internal struggles can be incredibly challenging to overcome because they require a level of introspection and honesty with yourself that many are not ready to handle.

Welcome to the heavyweight championship fight of your life: You vs You.

The Battle Within: You vs. You

I have a great love for movies; it's one of my favorite pastimes, whether in the theater or the comfort of my couch. Lately, it's been more of the latter, thanks to streaming services. One of my all-time favorite movie series is *Rocky*—I love all six of them. I've seen them countless times to the point where I know the majority of the lines. And just when I thought that nothing could top Rocky, they did a spin-off titled *Creed*. Sylvester Stallone, who plays the role of Rocky, reprises his character in *Creed* alongside Michael B. Jordan, introduced to us as the son of Apollo Creed, one of Rocky's biggest opponents turned friends.

In the first *Creed*, there's a poignant scene where Adonis is being trained by Rocky, and Rocky walks him over to the full-length mirrors at the gym and says to him, "Donnie, get into your stance. Make a small target and turn sideways." He then points to the mirror and says: "You see this guy here staring back at you? That's your toughest opponent. Every time you get into the ring that's who you're going against. I believe that in boxing and I do believe that in life."

Even though this is a quote from a movie, I believe it is just as powerful and true for real life. What Rocky was trying to explain to Adonis is that the greatest opponent he will ever face is within. The renowned Olympic gold medalist Jesse Owens once said, "The battles that count aren't the ones for gold medals. The struggles within yourself—the invisible, inevitable battles inside all of us—that's where it's at."

It starts within. Before you can confront any external opponents or opposition, you must first enter the arena of your soul and face you: your internal struggles, insecurities, inadequacies, low self-esteem, pride, mental anguish, and past trauma. You must grapple with unmet expectations, unfulfilled plans, and the tension between where you are presently and where you envision yourself being. You must come face-to-face with your failures, missed opportunities, and poor choices. And lastly, you must confront the labels and expectations that society and others have put on you, that you have come to accept; that standard you have come to measure (judge) yourself by.

Merely repeating affirmations daily isn't sufficient to change how you perceive yourself. While it may temporarily boost your outward confidence, deep down, those underlying feelings persist. Similarly, neglecting to address these internal struggles can sabotage the very opportunities you're praying for.

It's so easy to point the finger at others when things don't work out, but pointing the finger at ourselves often leads to dark places that we try to remedy with drinking, smoking, shopping, overeating, seeking attention, and seeking pleasure. It's a vicious cycle that many have learned to navigate over the years but never confront.

By no means am I saying it will be a walk in the park. I remember a few years ago when I made the decision to confront a toxic dating cycle. I got a book to help me navigate this. It was a seven-week journey with daily reading, reflecting, analyzing, and confronting patterns in my past and present. Let me tell you, there were mornings when I threw that book across the room because the soul work it required was more than I was willing to engage in. But I made the decision to stick with it, and it illuminated so many things that were influencing the decisions I was making. It was a hard and emotion-filled seven weeks. I had to confront parts of myself that had been distorted by trauma, rejection, shame, and insecurities. I had to face myself and challenge the negative perceptions I had developed that caused me to settle time and time again. I had to learn to see myself through a lens of truth and love, not through the distorted lens of past hurts. I won't lie and tell you that after, I started making all the right decisions, because I didn't. What I will say is that it made me more aware of the place I was making decisions from.

A few months ago, while I was unpacking boxes from my move, I came across the journal I had kept during that time. As I read through each entry, navigating the pain, disappointment, lack of hope, and hurt I was experiencing, all I could do was rejoice because I never thought I would experience anything other than what I was feeling during that time. Yet, the day I was reading that, my life had taken a 180-degree turn. I felt nothing but hope for my future, and the pain and disappointment are now lessons that I lean on as I navigate my dating life presently.

"One step at a time, one round at a time, one punch at a time." That's one of my other favorite lines from *Creed*. I know sometimes when we attempt to confront things in our lives, we tend to want to tackle them all at once, which in turn overwhelms us and eventually causes us to run away from a path of healing and wholeness. There is no such thing as a knockout in this fight. This is a soul fight, and you must address each area: mind, will, and emotions. To overcome in each area, you must engage deliberately and purposefully. Consider the following as you begin confronting yourself:

> ***Think about what you're thinking about*** – Your thoughts play a crucial role in your internal struggle, as the mind can be a battlefield in itself. Take a moment to truly reflect on

your thinking patterns. It's easy to get trapped in a loop of negative thinking. Often, these are the false narratives we tell ourselves, which stems more from our insecurities leading to a skewed self-perception. We sometimes blame this on other people, but the truth is their opinion is validated by our own self-perception giving it more merit than it deserves. Thinking about what you're thinking about is the first step to challenge and question these damaging thought patterns and beliefs that undermine your confidence and self-worth. Next, identify a Scripture, quote, or affirmation that you can repeat when these thoughts start to resurface. Here's an example of each:

- **Scripture:** *"I let go of every thought that doesn't align with God's truth, and I focus on what brings me closer to Him."* – 2 Corinthians 10:5

- **Quote:** *"You are braver than you believe, stronger than you seem, and smarter than you think."* – A. A. Milne.

- **Affirmation:** *"I am enough. I choose to believe in my worth. I release thoughts that do not serve me."*

Be intentional – Embrace the discipline and determination required to confront past and present trauma, overcome obstacles, and face daily challenges. Pray. Set clear goals, make thoughtful choices, and take deliberate steps to unpack and offload the weight you've been carrying around. Remember, you don't have to do this alone. Identify a trusted friend with the capacity to support you through this and/or seek the help of a trained professional.

Don't be ruled by your emotions – Emotions are a natural part of life and certainly womanhood, but they shouldn't dictate your actions or decisions. Allow yourself to feel without being ruled by your emotions. The best way to deal with them is to first recognize them, and then take a moment to introspect so you can understand where they're coming from before you choose how to respond. When you're not ruled by your emotions, you can navigate difficult situations with a clear mind, making decisions that are in your best interest rather than reacting impulsively.

You won't conquer everything in one go. This journey will require time, patience, openness, and love. Instead of focusing on pleasing everyone, prioritize your inner development and growth so you can unapologetically be yourself. People will always have opinions and try to impose them on you, but what they think and believe about you shouldn't define who you are. While it's important not to dismiss all feedback, we should learn to measure others' opinions against the truth of God's word.

You don't have to be perfect, and you don't have to meet anyone's expectations. Give yourself grace as you navigate these obstacles. Remember, it's YOU vs YOU—the greatest battle you'll ever face. But I promise, you'll emerge as a much stronger, more authentic version of yourself.

An Even Greater Battle: You vs. God

The next greatest battle of your life is a spiritual one, between you and God. Specifically, it's between the self you aspire to be and the self God is calling you to become. Earlier, I discussed the transformation process that requires you to change how you see yourself, leading to changes in how you live your life. To take it a step further, there should be a desire to align your way of living with God's plan for your life. This often conflicts with our own desires and goals. For some, the battle emerge because you struggle to see yourselves the way God sees you. For others, it's the struggle to embrace the transformation and growth that God is taking you through. We see this in Genesis 32: 22–30 with Jacob as he wrestles with God.

Jacob had long lived in a manner he found fitting, a manner that worked for him but it was contrary to the will of God for his life. Jacob was a schemer and a trickster. Jacob came out of his mother's womb grasping the heel of his brother. He took his brother's birthright in exchange for a meal. He then tricked his father into giving him a blessing that wasn't his. And now Jacob is between a rock and a hard place that was brought on by his own actions. He is alone and he finds himself in the greatest fight of his life but this fight is different from the other fights he had in the past because this fight would change his life forever.

The event takes place as Jacob prepares to reunite with his brother, Esau, whom he had deceived many years earlier. Jacob is filled with fear and anxiety about the encounter, as Esau had previously vowed to kill him.

That night, Jacob gathered his family—his two wives, two female servants, and eleven sons—and led them across the ford of the Jabbok. After ensuring they were safely across, along with all their possessions, Jacob was left alone on the far side of the stream.

Suddenly, a mysterious man appeared and began to wrestle with Jacob. The struggle continued until the first light of dawn began to break. Despite the man's efforts, he could not overpower Jacob. In a decisive move, the man touched Jacob's hip socket, causing it to be dislocated.

As dawn approached, the man told Jacob to let him go, but Jacob refused. He insisted, "I will not let you go unless you bless me." The man then asked, "What is your name?" Jacob answered, "Jacob." The man replied, "Your name will no longer be Jacob, but Israel, because you have struggled with God and with humans and have overcome."

Jacob then asked for the man's name, but the man responded, "Why do you ask my name?" He then blessed Jacob and departed. Jacob named the place Peniel, which means "face of God," explaining, "It is because I saw God face to face, yet my life was spared."

The Surrender

Jacob isn't engaged in an ordinary scuffle—he's grappling with God Himself. Jacob acknowledges this in verse 30, naming the place Peniel, saying, "I have seen God face to face, and my life is preserved." You might wonder, why would God descend from heaven, take on the form of a man, and confront Jacob? And why would God, the healer, restorer, and giver of life, intentionally injure Jacob's hip?

What may seem like an unconventional approach to us, is God's deliberate strategy. The battle symbolized more than just Jacob's struggle with the Divine, it was a profound wrestle with his own identity and destiny. No longer defined by the name *Jacob*, which means "deceiver," he emerged transformed, as one who had wrestled with God and prevailed.

Yet, I believe God broke Jacob's hip to capture his attention. Jacob only realized he was wrestling with God after his hip was broken, which brought about his surrender. In the fight with yourself, I told you that you would have to go round by round battling the things on the inside in order to triumph. However, this fight is different. Unlike other fights, the way to triumph in this fight is to surrender.

It's interesting that when we hear this story, many often focus on Jacob's bold declaration, "I won't let you go until you bless me," but overlook the significance of his refusal to surrender. Despite God's directive to let Him go as dawn approached, Jacob clung on, insisting on receiving God's blessing. Isn't that like many of us? We resist following God's guidance yet still expect God's provisions. We want to live life on our terms, yet still anticipate

God's protection. We hesitate to fully surrender, yet we demand God's blessings.

God won't do what He wants to do until you surrender. Sure God can do it, but He won't. And yes, just like with Jacob, God has ways of getting our attention because God loves you too much to leave you on the path you're on, knowing that there is a better path. How many things must happen for God to get your attention? How many things must happen for you to stop and surrender?

Understand that the fight is not for God's entertainment or for God to throw His weight around. The fight is to bring you to complete and total surrender, where you acknowledge that you don't know it all and you don't have it all together. However, you trust your Creator, the author, and finisher of your faith, the one who holds you in the palm of His hand. You trust that in uncertainty or certainty, God knows best.

Pause, Consider, Take Action

1. Who is the "self" that you aspire to be, and what are the motivations behind these aspirations?

2. In what areas of life are you resisting change or growth, especially when it comes to aligning with God's plan (purpose)?

3. How can you actively cultivate a mindset of surrender and openness to God's plan, even when it diverges from your own expectations?

4. Reflect on the ways you may be overly critical of yourself, judging yourself by unrealistic standards or the opinions of others. Consider how fear and self-doubt might be distorting

your self-perception, as described in Numbers 13:33. In what areas of your life do you feel like a "grasshopper in your own eyes"? How can you begin to shift your focus to see yourself through a more truthful and positive lens?

____

____

____

____

____

CHAPTER 4

In Community
Part One

I recently took a Christian education class that was truly impactful. During one session, our professor prompted us with the following sentence: "If I was a part of the body, I would be the ___ because ___." As my classmates shared their responses, attributing different body parts to their varying gifts and abilities, I found myself mentally listing various body parts, trying to determine which one I could comfortably identify with. When my turn came, I said, "If I were a part of the body, I would be the fingers because I like to help things move."

Since that moment, I've been reflecting on the significance of each part of the body and how it contributes to our overall health and optimal functioning. This reflection also made me think deeply about the concept of community. Just like the body relies on each part, a person's well-being and success are heavily influenced by their community. On the other hand, just as a weak or dysfunctional part of the body can impact the entire system, a toxic or unsupportive community can hinder an individual's growth and well-being. It's a reminder of the importance of surrounding ourselves with positive influences and fostering strong connections.

In our community, we encounter a diverse array of individuals, ranging from family members, whether by blood or choice, to friends, colleagues, church members, mentors, teachers, classmates, and even your hair stylist. Each person contributes to the dynamic fabric of our community, wielding varying degrees of influence in our lives. You might question the significance of someone such as your hair stylist, in shaping your life. Consider the countless conversations you've shared while in the styling chair and the advice imparted by your stylist over the years. Also, think about the times you altered your hairstyles based on their suggestions. Whether consciously acknowledged or not, every member of our community leaves an imprint on our journey, whether it be profound or subtle, positive or negative, or as a lesson to heed. Our community is instrumental in shaping our journey.

Family Ties

I could probably write an entire book about family dynamics and their profound impact on our lives. Our families often lay the foundation for how we interact with others and perceive the world. These early experiences shape our understanding of trust, love, conflict, and communication, all of which influence how we build and nurture relationships outside the home. The way we approach friendships, seek mentorship, and engage with others often reflects the dynamics we experienced growing up. In essence, our families are the first communities we belong to, setting the tone for how we engage with all others.

While family can provide a sense of belonging and support, it can also present challenges that test our resilience. Reflecting on these dynamics helps us to be more intentional in our current relationships, allowing us to build communities that genuinely support our growth and well-being. For example, someone who grew up in a family with open communication may find it easier to form similar relationships in adulthood, while someone who experienced rejection might struggle with trust or intimacy.

It is often those closest to us who have the potential to hurt us the most. Conflict in any relationship can alter not only the dynamic but also our own character. I have had negative experiences with family that have made me cynical at times. Many of us can relate—whether it's dealing with rejection, enduring a hostile environment, or facing a relative who always seems to have something negative to say. These experiences can cloud our vision and shape our perspective on life.

However, we are not confined by our family dynamics. As we grow, we have the power to choose which aspects of our familial experiences to embrace and which to let go of. This discernment is vital for creating a life and community that truly reflect our values and aspirations. If this means stepping away from certain family traditions or distancing ourselves from certain family members, that is OK. Sometimes, we need to consciously remove ourselves from toxic patterns, even if it causes discomfort or friction. This doesn't mean intentionally creating conflict, but rather not being afraid to step away from what brings us harm.

It's easy to focus on the negative, especially if our family relationships have been challenging. However, it's equally important to recognize the strengths and gifts that have come from our families. A balanced perspective allows us to appreciate our experiences and decide which parts of our family dynamics to build on or break free from, creating space for our own growth and healing.

What About Your Friends?

In 1992, the girl group TLC released a song titled "What About Your Friends." The chorus, which many of us can remember belting out every time the song played on the radio, went like this:

> *"What about your friends?*
> *Will they stand their ground?*
> *Will they let you down? hey yay*
> *What about your friends?*
> *Are they gonna be low down?*
> *Will they ever be around?*
> *Or will they turn their backs on you?"*

I was only eleven years old when this song was released, and back then, I had no idea what its deeper meaning was. At that age, I held on to the belief that my closest friends would remain by my side forever, living in the house next door with the matching picket fence, while our families shared a strong bond—best friends for life. Little did I know how mistaken I was.

As a kid, a fight with your best friend seemed like it was the end of the world. But you worked through it and promised each other you would not let anything come between your friendship ever again. You even made friendship bracelets to seal the deal. Then boys came along, and interests evolved. Then college or career choice. Eventually, you find your way back together, grow apart, or remain cordial but no longer best friends.

As a parent, I'm observing this unfold from the outside, watching my teenage son as his friendship circles change from his early years to the present. These changes are influenced by several factors: changing schools, relocation, maturity, and evolving interests and hobbies. While he's maintained a few friends throughout the years, the nature of their relationships has still shifted. The reality is that all of our friendship circles will evolve; some will be strengthened, some will be redefined, and others will end. And that's OK. Not everyone is meant to be in your life for a lifetime.

Types of Friendships

In my early twenties, I learned that people come into our lives for a reason, a season, or a lifetime. It took me almost twenty years of experiencing hurt, disappointment, and frustration to fully understand this concept.

Reason friendships are those whose time in your life was brief but impactful. They may have taught you a valuable lesson or helped you out of a tough situation—or you might have done the same for them. For example, someone going through a painful divorce joins a spin class and makes a friend there. This friend motivates them to keep pushing, calls them when they miss a class, and looks out for them. With this friend's encouragement, she begins to find her way again. Eventually, the class ends, and they commit to meeting up regularly to catch up but are unable to keep that promise. Over time, the friendship fades.

An alternative ending is that the encouraging friend keeps calling, texting, and trying to meet up, but it always seems like the person is busy or doesn't have time for them. This hurts the encouraging friend because she felt they had a bond worth nurturing.

A reason friendship, though often short and impactful, can hurt just as much as a seasonal friendship. I learned this the hard way. The mistake I kept making—which most of us do—was not recognizing reason friendships for what they were and trying to force them to run longer than their natural course. When someone has such a profound impact on your life, it is almost impossible to imagine a world in which they are no longer a part of your life. However, trying to keep a reason friendship longer than its purpose, almost always ends up breeding toxicity. Suddenly, this *amazing* person begins to wear you down and you find yourself having to work ten times harder just to keep the friendship. Trust me, this becomes exhausting very quickly.

But it goes both ways. I used to work hard to stay in people's life. I didn't recognize I was only a reason friend to them, so I'd put in extra effort, be more intentional, call and text way more than they ever did, and each time, I'd be left feeling ignored. I never understood what I was doing wrong or why they were shutting me out. I would eventually come to learn that they were in my life for a reason.

Remember, the reason friendships exist is to serve a purpose. Even if the experience was challenging, you likely learned a lot about yourself and how to navigate similar situations in the future.

Seasonal friendships, on the other hand, last longer but still have a time limit. Friends from college or work are good examples. While the friendship may fade after a certain period, the experiences and lessons remain. These friendships can end amicably or not. They could last as little as a few months or last for several years, which is why they hurt so much when it's over. Can you imagine spending years of your life making memories with someone, and then they move on?

I had several seasonal friendships in my twenties. People often say your twenties are a time of exploration—a period when you try new things and discover who you truly are. During these years, it's also common to experience many seasonal friendships that come and go as you evolve.

These bonds are often hard to walk away from because they feel so deep and lasting, making it seem like these people will be in your life forever. However, as time goes on, people often grow in different directions, leaving friendships to navigate life's rapid changes. While some friendships survive, others come to an end.

For some, these friendships become a crutch, and they hold on to the familiar even when it's clear the relationship has run its course.

It's natural to feel heartbroken when these friendships end. There's a profound sense of loss when an important chapter of your life closes so suddenly. But despite the pain, these experiences are also beautiful. They teach us resilience, adaptability, and the importance of cherishing the moments we have.

Even though you might end things on a upsetting note, the focus, however, should be on the positive impact the relationship had on you. Seasonal friends can be friends you've known for a lifetime but cannot be confused with lifetime friends.

Lifetime friendships are those that stand by you through various stages of life, providing unwavering support and receiving it in return. These friendships require time, openness, honesty, and mutual respect to truly thrive. When you meet such a friend, you may not recognize them as a lifelong companion right away. Sometimes, it may surprise you—they might not have been someone you expected to connect with at all. Or perhaps you initially saw them as a seasonal friend, only to realize later that they are a lifetime friend. It's important to note that having a lifetime friend doesn't mean you spend a lot of time together or are in constant communication; it's about the quality of the time you do share.

I never thought I'd consider someone I don't see regularly a close friend, but here I am. Adulthood has taught me that you don't need to be in constant contact to maintain a strong friendship. I used to think that a good friend was someone who called every day and knew every detail of my life. But as I've grown older, I've come to appreciate the friends who check in after weeks or even months. Our priorities have shifted, and it no longer makes sense to be on the phone all the time, talking about everything and nothing (though I still have one or two friends with whom I do that). Still, I knew they would be there for me in a heartbeat if I needed them. Different cities, different coasts, none of that matters. What truly matters is how deeply we value each other.

My friend Stephanie and I met in our early twenties at a young adult conference in New York City. She was there for the summer, and I had just moved to the city. We quickly bonded over our shared passions for fashion, personal development, and ministry. That summer, we navigated the streets of NYC in four-inch heels (these days, I stick to flats, but if you ask Stephanie, she'll be in heels until the day she dies). We explored the city, got to know each other, and shared our hopes and dreams, laying a strong foundation for a friendship that has continued to grow over the years. Although we don't talk every day or see each other often, we always encourage and support one another through texts, voice notes, or quick calls. Depending on the season, our communication may be more or less frequent, but Stephanie has remained an integral part of my life to this day.

I also met one of my closest friends, Tasha at work over ten years ago. I remember telling her that I felt like we would be friends for a long time. Her response was always, "Oh no, I've had the same friend circle since I was a kid. You and I will only be friends while we're at this job. As soon as either of us leave, our friendship will end." Of all the friends that we made in that time, she and I are the only ones who continue to be close friends today. I remind her of that every chance I get.

You never know when you will meet a lifetime friend. It's important that you give your friendships a chance to blossom before you limit them to a season or even a location. So many people have the same response as Tasha, "I've had the same friend circle since I was a kid," until life takes them elsewhere and they learn that some of those friendships they tried to protect so fiercely were actually seasonal.

Friendships are a beautiful thing and can greatly enhance your life. It requires ongoing effort and nurturing to sustain and bloom. Healthy friendships should be open and honest and allow for each other to share their feelings without tension and grudges. However, you must commit yourself to making friendships work. You must put in the time, care, and effort to make it work. You must be vulnerable and build trust. At the same time, you must be gracious and forgiving.

Beware of holding on to reason and seasonal friendships hoping to turn them into lifelong friendships even after their time has expired. While you might still consider yourselves friends, the relationship can become toxic, damaging, and a hindrance to your personal growth (overtly or covertly). Start paying attention to your friendships. Learn to categorize and accept the category a friend might be in. Don't try to extend someone's time in your life, especially if the relationship has become or is showing signs of becoming toxic. And remember, whether a friendship lasts briefly, for a season, or for a lifetime, there's often something beneficial gained—even if it's just the wisdom to recognize warning signs.

Friendship Grief

I would be remiss if I didn't talk about the grief we experience when a friendship changes or ends. We often feel the feelings, but we don't necessarily know what to do with them. First, it's important to note that the opposite of a friend is not an enemy. It's a person who no longer holds the same significance they once did.

Friendship grief is a unique kind of sorrow that many of us aren't prepared for. We're taught to expect grief when we lose a loved one to death, but the loss of a friendship can be just as painful, if not more so because it's often a silent grief. It's a gradual process, where one day you realize that the person who once knew you better than anyone else has drifted away, and you're left with memories that feel both comforting and haunting.

The stages of grief—denial, anger, bargaining, depression, and acceptance—can apply to friendships just as they do to romantic relationships or the loss of a loved one. You may cycle through these stages multiple times, and that's normal. You might find yourself replaying old memories, questioning what went wrong, or blaming yourself.

Remember, it's not about blaming yourself or the other person. Sometimes, friendships simply run their course. It's about understanding that change is a natural part of life and that it's OK to feel the pain that comes with it. Grief is a nonlinear process. You might experience these stages in a different order, or revisit them multiple times. There's no right or wrong way to grieve a friendship.

The hardest part about friendship grief is that it often goes unrecognized or simply overlooked. You'll find that the people around you don't offer words of comfort or even acknowledge that you have experienced loss. Mourning the death of a friendship does not fit into the traditional narrative of what grief looks like, even though it can be just as heartbreaking.

However, no matter what, you have to allow yourself the time and space to grieve. You have to allow yourself to feel your feelings and accept what you are going through. Facing the pain with kindness and understanding is a crucial step toward healing and finding peace.

Change Is a Part of Life

My friend Tasha and I had been going to the same nail technician for years. Tasha had been a client since high school and later introduced me to her. We were both loyal customers, visiting our nail tech regularly. Over time, we noticed a decline in the quality of service she provided. She seemed more focused on accommodating as many clients as possible and began neglecting the quality of her work.

We waited it out for almost two years, hoping it was just a phase and things would improve. However, the situation only worsened, which was evidenced by the service we received and the end result of our nails. Occasionally, after our appointments, Tasha and I would call each other to vent about our frustrations. Despite our dissatisfaction, we hesitated to find a new nail technician, fearing the inconvenience and uncertainty of change. Eventually, we reached our breaking point and began searching for alternatives.

I decided to try a different nail salon altogether. The idea of change was daunting, but we had settled for subpar service for far too long. What was even worse was realizing, upon exploring other options, how undervalued we had been as customers. We realized that we didn't have to accept such a low standard of care because there were many options available, we just had to be open to them.

Many of you have likely experienced shifts in your community, yet you have ignored, complained about, or underestimated these changes. Beneath the surface, tensions are brewing in your community. Overdue conversations are being replaced with outward pleasantries and inward resentment. You may overlook these simmering problems because you fear conflict and change. However, what you fail to realize is that change has already begun. The way you once interacted has shifted, as has your perception of the individual's significance in your life. If you haven't realized it yet, let me be the one to tell you: what you fear is already in motion, so you might as well address it.

Oftentimes, these issues don't just impact one relationship; they seep into others as well. It's like an active volcano, it might not have erupted as yet but there is a lot of activity happening beneath the surface and once it reaches the point of eruption, it impacts everything in its path.

By addressing these issues, you might reach a mutual under-standing or amicably sever relationships that no longer serve you. However, if left unaddressed, these issues will inevitably escalate to a point of no return.

As adults, making new friends often requires vulnerability and active effort, which can be daunting. This might cause us to hesitate to truly evaluate the relationships within our community, fearing what it might mean if there is a shift or a necessary ending.

It's easy to cling to what we know, even if it's no longer serving us. We might fear loneliness, judgment, or the disruption of our routines. These fears can create a sense of complacency, preventing us from seeking out deeper connections or addressing unhealthy dynamics within our existing relationships.

Tasha and I wasted two years on a nail tech who was giving us nothing but frustration because of familiarity. We were so afraid of change that we accepted a subpar service just because the solution required us to step out of our comfort zone.

No matter which angle you view it from, change is intimidating, especially when friendships are intertwined with our sense of identity and belonging. It's easier to keep things as they are, to avoid the discomfort of change, even if it means staying in relationships that might have even become toxic. We often find it easier to say, "Oh, that's just how___ is," instead of addressing the toxicity and redefining the friendship.

Yes, change can be scary, and not knowing what will happen next can be unsettling, but peace is priceless. Peace means not tossing and turning all night because of an unaddressed issue. It's about showing up authentically without altering yourself because of someone else's presence. It's acknowledging that you no longer share the same interests and being honest about it. Peace is also about avoiding heated, below-the-belt arguments that leave you in tears and in pain. And finally, it's about allowing relationships to shift, change, and even end when they're supposed to.

Change in our community is necessary and inevitable, and while it can be challenging, it also brings opportunities for growth and empowerment. Embracing change in our community can lead to the creation of deeper, more meaningful relationships and a stronger sense of community.

Navigating Mentor Relationships

Mentorship is highly valued for its ability to guide us through life's journey. Yet, while I deeply believe in its importance, I will admit that my experiences have left me with mixed feelings about fully embracing it. On the one hand, I've been blessed with amazing mentors who have imparted invaluable lessons, supporting me personally, professionally, and spiritually. Their belief in me has opened doors and shaped my path in profound ways.

Yet, I've also encountered mentors whose intentions were not as pure. Some seemed threatened by my potential success, attempting to hinder my progress. Others placed limits on my growth, discouraging me from exploring new opportunities. It often felt like there was an unspoken rule that I shouldn't surpass them or aspire to a level that they hadn't attained.

True mentorship, as I see it, should empower us to reach our full potential without being constrained by personal limitations or ego. When seeking or embracing a mentor, don't do so simply because you aspire to be like them. What I've found is that one-third of the people we aspire to be like are living a facade and not truly what they display. Another third is looking at you the same way you're looking at them, wishing they had what you have. The remaining third is comprised of genuine individuals who can offer sincere guidance and support. That's the pool you want to choose from and have guiding you as you move along your journey.

If you're assuming the role of a mentor, it's crucial to examine your motives beforehand. Make sure you're genuinely dedicated to fostering the growth and development of the individual you're mentoring. Your guidance should be rooted in authenticity and a sincere desire to see them thrive. Remember, true mentorship is not about ego or control but about empowering others to unlock their full potential and navigate their journey with confidence and integrity. Be open to the relationship being reciprocal, while you may have the experience and expertise, there are always things you can learn from your mentee. This mutual exchange fosters respect and builds trust between you both.

A successful mentor creates a safe and supportive environment where the mentee feels encouraged to explore, experiment, and make mistakes. It involves active listening, providing constructive feedback, and sharing your own experiences without imposing your perspective. It's not just about what you think is best, but finding the best solutions and opportunities for your mentee. By offering guidance while allowing the mentee to find their own path, you empower them to develop their unique strengths and problem-solving skills.

When you're driving in an unfamiliar location, the first thing you do is turn on your GPS and trust it to guide you back to the right street you need to be on. What the GPS doesn't do is get behind your wheel and drive the car for you. It offers you different routes and reroutes you if you take a wrong turn, all with the singular purpose of getting you on the right track to your destination. This is essentially what a mentor is supposed to do.

Remember, a mentor is a guide, not a dictator. Your role is to provide insights, offer perspectives, and share your experiences. Ultimately, the decisions and actions belong to the mentee. I have seen too many mentors impose their choices and beliefs on mentees as though they're trying to create duplicates of themselves. You cannot empower someone else by taking away their sense of agency.

Pause, Consider, Take Action

1. Think of all the individuals who make up your current community. Write down the name and the value each person brings to your life. If you are unable to think of their current value, ask yourself, "Has this person overstayed their welcome in my life, especially in my close community?"

2. How have you personally adapted to change within your community? Share a specific example where you were initially resistant but later embraced the change. What factors influenced your acceptance, and what impact did this change have on both your community and yourself?

3. Think about a mentor throughout your life. How did that person become your mentor? Looking back, do you believe your mentor was genuine and provided sincere guidance? How did their guidance impact your personal and professional growth?

CHAPTER 5

In Community - Part Two: In Silence

When I started outlining this book, I knew I couldn't talk about community without talking about the painful things that occur within our communities. Unfortunately, ugliness can appear even in environments that are meant to be nurturing and encourage trust.

When I was around twelve years old, I was molested by my afterschool director in his truck every time he dropped me home. I remember feeling uncomfortable and trying to make sense of what was happening. I eventually quit the afterschool program, never explaining to my mother the reason. A few years later, I was at a church youth camp, and we were broken into two sections by gender for one of our morning sessions. It was a closed-door, question-and-answer session that allowed the girls to write their questions on paper and drop them in a basket. I remember one question from a girl who was being molested by someone in her household, asking what she should do. The bravery of the girl who wrote that question led to several others submitting similar questions or describing similar scenarios. I was in tears. I bawled for hours. Even after the session, I sat with one of the youth leaders and cried profusely, never talking or sharing about my experience, just crying.

That day, I realized that I was not alone, and I didn't have to be ashamed. Yet, I didn't have the courage to confront the situation fearing how my mom would respond and how this individual, who at the time was a prominent figure, would handle it. It was then that I learned what it meant to move in silence. Unfortunately, that would not be the last time I had to navigate inappropriate, harmful, or uncomfortable situations in a supposedly nurturing and trustworthy environment. And while I eventually removed myself from those situations, I did so in silence.

There are many reasons that we, particularly as women, have moved or are currently moving in silence. Moving in silence is a survival method to navigate uncomfortable spaces and situations. This includes spaces where someone else has power and influence that could be wielded over you. Instead of confronting your discomfort, you may choose to ignore it, make excuses to alleviate it, or even participate in normalizing the situation.

I once had a supervisor who regularly took credit for my work, despite appearing supportive and encouraging. She consistently assigned me the bulk of the workload while taking credit for my efforts. This caused me to initially move in silence; at first, I was in shock, and then I just wanted to get the work done because it impacted my entire department. I didn't speak up until almost four months later when I felt comfortable enough in the environment to believe that my experience mattered.

I'm not here to tell you to speak up or confront the individual or the environment in which you are moving in silence. And while you can choose to do both those things, it should be a personal choice and should never be made by coercion. Whether anyone agrees with it or not, the reason you move in silence is for your protection and to protect your peace. It's to ensure that your reputation stays intact and you don't move from being a victim to a villain. In some instances, it's to ensure that you still have a paycheck to keep a roof over your head, as well as a whole host of other reasons known only to you and do not need to be explained to anyone. I know this is an unpopular route for a topic like this as we are in an era of trending hashtags and encouragement to "speak your truth." And while I support individuals who decide to take that route, I also stand with those who decide to move in silence. We know all too well that even with the hashtags and the marketing campaigns, women are not protected in our society. We are used, then misused, then ignored or forgotten about.

If you ever make the choice to move forward in silence, ensure that you have the proper support in place to help you navigate the silence. Supports such as a trusted friend, a therapist, or a support group. **Most importantly, make a plan to remove yourself from the person and/or environment that is causing you to move in silence. Then, execute that plan. While moving in silence is a choice, it should only be temporary, it cannot be a permanent state of being.**

Moving in silence can also occur within our relationships and friendship circles, but in this case, the power being wielded is the relationship/friendship itself. It's more nuanced and complex because of the bond, the shared history, and the fear of disrupting those connections. The fear of rejection, isolation, or betrayal can be paralyzing. However, clinging to a friendship out of obligation or fear can be detrimental to your overall well-being.

Sometimes, our expectations create an environment where expressing dissatisfaction or setting boundaries in friendships feels selfish or disruptive, leading us to stay silent. This silence can foster an imbalanced power dynamic where you avoid disagreement or conflict to keep the peace. You might find this happening more often in your life than you realize. It often starts with letting small issues slide, which makes it harder to have open and honest conversations. Once you let something go, it becomes easier to pretend you're OK with it. This often results in emotional exhaustion and a one-sided dynamic that isn't sustainable.

Remember, you don't have to sacrifice your emotional well-being just to maintain a relationship/friendship. Staying silent out of fear of losing the relationship only deepens the cycle of people-pleasing and self-neglect. At some point, breaking the silence through a heartfelt conversation with your friend or by taking steps to distance yourself from a relationship that no longer supports your well-being is essential. While it may be painful, it is important to remember that letting go of relationships that no longer serve you creates space for new, healthier connections and personal growth.

Check Yourself

I would be remiss if I did not ask you to ensure that you are not the reason someone else is moving in silence. Part of being in a community is being mindful of how our words and actions impact those around us. Often perpetrators are self-centered and so enamored with their own selves that they neglect to see how their actions are impacting those around them. And frankly, in some instances, they don't care. Stop, and consider how you interact with those in your community. This is even more vital for those in positions of leadership.

On our journey through life, the role of community cannot be overstated. It serves as a source of support, love, and comfort, offering solace in times of need and celebration in moments of joy. However, the dynamics within a community are multifaceted, sometimes presenting unexpected challenges alongside the fulfillment of shared experiences. We need one another, but that need should never be abused. Everyone deserves to feel seen, heard, and valued.

As you navigate your relationships, aim to create an environment where everyone feels heard and valued. It's easy to get wrapped up in your own feelings and how others are affecting you, but remember that relationships are a two-way street. Always be open to honest dialogue, even if it feels uncomfortable. Avoid being the reason someone feels they have to stay silent.

Be mindful of how you treat others and regularly check in with yourself, especially if you sense a change in your relationships. Being part of a community means taking responsibility not only for your own actions but also for their impact on others. Though silence is sometimes necessary, I want you to know our actions, whether silent or loud, can inspire positive change in every relationship you nurture. We still need each other, and we need to take care of each other.

Pause, Consider, Take Action

1. Reflect on a time when you faced challenges within your community.
   - How did you navigate those challenges?

- Did you find yourself moving in silence, or did you address the issues directly?

- What were the factors that influenced your decision, and what did you learn from the experience?

2. If you find yourself presently in silence, write a plan for how you can remove yourself from the situation, separate yourself

from the person, or both. Include who you can look to for support as you navigate this time.

3. Consider your actions and how you interact with those in your community.

Intermission: Checking In

Hey lady,

Before we go any further, I want to take a moment to check in with you, especially since the last chapter may have felt a bit heavy.

When I set out to write this book, my goals were clear: to be both authentic and intentional. I wanted each chapter, topic, and personal story to reflect my own experiences while speaking to the diverse journeys of women from all walks of life. I didn't want to offer advice on how to live your life without ensuring it came from a place of genuine reflection and care. To achieve this, I had to delve into the same places I'm inviting you to explore.

The last chapter, in particular, took me longer to write. It required me to revisit and share experiences I had long kept buried. I did this because I believe that sharing my truth can help you confront and release your own, guiding you toward acknowledgment and healing. Please know that you are not alone—many women are walking this path alongside you.

This book was inspired by a Galentine's event I hosted in February 2023 called Pink and Red Conversations with a group of phenomenal women. We explored three key themes: Live, Love, Lead. We defined these concepts and examined our lives through those definitions. It was a profound, emotional, and revealing conversation.

Additionally, when I began writing, I formed a group of women from varying ages and backgrounds to review the chapters and share how the book resonated with them. Their insights helped ensure the book is relatable and transformative.

My hope is that this experience will be as enriching and empowering for you as it has been for me and the women I mentioned. Remember, this is a journey, not a sprint; it's a steady walk toward growth and self-discovery. I encourage you to take your time to sit with and answer the reflection questions and process everything thoroughly. You will get a lot more out of the book by doing so.

Now, take a moment to pause, breathe deeply, and process at your own pace. Continue to the next chapter whenever you feel ready.

Warmly,

Tanna

CHAPTER 6

How Are You Living?

In my daily juggle of professional, academic, and personal commitments, I'm also a ride-share driver for my thirteen-year-old son, Caden. Or at least, that's what he believes. Each afternoon, I'm typically in the school pickup line by 3:15, just before classes let out at 3:20. Occasionally, a meeting runs over, delaying my arrival until around 3:35. And then there are times when I run errands before picking him up and I finish early, putting me in the pickup line around 3:00.

One particular week, I found myself arriving earlier than usual for a few days. It wasn't until Caden voiced his desire for me to return to the regular pickup time that I realized the impact of these variations. He explained how arriving early meant he had to rush straight to the car, missing out on time with his friends. Arriving later meant he often found himself alone, as his peers had already left. Caden expressed that coming at my regular time gave him a few minutes to "live," as he puts it. Those extra minutes were a time free from the interruptions of teachers, administrators, or parents, where he could catch up, laugh, and simply be himself. I'm sure he could do this during lunchtime, but we won't go there (*insert side-eye*).

His words sparked a reflection within me. Did I have such a moment in my day, where I could truly "live"? And if so, how could I extend that time beyond the fleeting ten minutes Caden craved?

Another insight I gained from my conversation with Caden is that everyone has their own unique interpretation of what it means to truly live life to the fullest. When I speak of living, I'm referring to seizing every opportunity and experiencing joy in its purest form. Yet, this concept varies greatly from person to person. For some, it's a job they love, spending quality time with family and friends. For others, it might be philanthropic work—helping others and finding joy in making a difference. It can be traveling the world, checking things off a bucket list, reaching the pinnacle of your career, or indulging in things that make you happy. The paths may differ, but the ultimate goal remains constant: embracing life with vigor and intentionality.

"There's one certainty in life—we don't choose when we depart this world, but we do have a say in how we choose to live it."

I can't recall where I first heard these words, but they've stayed with me ever since. Each morning, we awaken to a new day, a new opportunity to embrace life. We're uncertain of what lies ahead, but what we do know is that we have the present. The here and now. The question is, how are we seizing the moment?

Many people plan extensively for their future. They work hard to set up the life they eventually want to have and spend the majority of their life working on that only for it to be short-lived. My nail technician told me about a client of hers who recently made some drastic changes in her life. This person and her husband worked hard from the time they graduated from college. Through their hard work, they were able to purchase a house and get to a comfortable place of living. They then started making all these retirement plans. They sacrificed vacations and time with family and friends, all to build the future they desired. When they finally got to retirement age and were about to embark on the adventures they were longing for, her husband was diagnosed with cancer and died not long after. All the things they had put off to get to this point and now he was unable to do them. This experience changed the lady's mindset and she made the decision then and there to start living fully. She started taking vacations every other month, discovering her passions and indulging in them. She expressed to my nail tech that her only regret is that she didn't start living sooner because if she had, she would have been able to enjoy some of these experiences with her husband.

Stories like these, along with my own experiences of loss, have profoundly shaped my perspective on life. I've come to embrace the mantra, "Prepare for tomorrow, but live for today." It's a delicate balance, striving for a secure future while cherishing the moments we have in the present. After all, tomorrow is never guaranteed, and every moment we spend focusing on the future is a moment lost in the present. So, I encourage you to take a step back, reevaluate your priorities, and savor the beauty of each moment. Embrace life with open arms, for it is in the present that we find true fulfillment and joy.

Breathe Life into Your Life

I am fully aware that life can be overwhelming. For some, it feels like life has taken so much from you that you have no more energy left. You might feel like living is a chore, barely making it from day to day. It's not because you don't want to keep going, but because you're so exhausted from how life has beaten you down in the past that you feel like you don't have much left to give to the present. I want you to know that your feelings are valid. Living doesn't mean ignoring your past experiences or present reality; it means moving forward despite them.

I don't know you personally, so I can't pretend to understand what you've been through or what you're currently experiencing. However, I want to offer you a word of encouragement to lift your spirits: YOU CAN LIVE AGAIN! I know this because I learned the principle of living from one of my favorite Bible stories, the story of Ezekiel in the Valley of Dry Bones.

In Ezekiel 37, God leads Ezekiel to a valley filled with dry, bleached bones—an image of utter desolation and hopelessness. He walks him through the valley surrounded by the remnants of life lost. It is in this barren place that God delivers a profound message of hope to Ezekiel: even in the most desolate places, God can bring forth life.

As they walk through the valley, God asks Ezekiel a thought-provoking question: "Can these bones live?" Ezekiel responds, "Sovereign Lord, only you know."

This exchange always brings a smile to my face while raising several questions. Why would God ask a question He already knows the answer to? Was it Ezekiel's wit that led him to respond this way, or was he acknowledging his belief in God's power and sovereignty? Regardless, this dialogue sets the stage for the powerful lesson that follows.

God commands Ezekiel to prophesy, to speak a prophetic message. Ezekiel obeys, demonstrating a crucial principle: We can speak life into our circumstances, no matter how bleak they may seem. As a result of his obedience, Ezekiel witnesses a miraculous transformation in the valley. We too can experience new life and restoration in our own lives; however, we must understand that it is a step-by-step process. Note that God often works through processes, teaching us patience and trust in His timing.

First, God tells Ezekiel to prophesy to the bones. As he does, the bones begin to come together, flesh grows, and skin wraps around them. Yet, the bodies remain lifeless. Then, God instructs Ezekiel to prophesy to the lifeless bodies and speak breath into them. At this point, the bodies arise as a mighty army.

God then commands Ezekiel to prophesy to the winds, calling forth the breath of life. Reminding us that no matter how lifeless our situations may seem, God can breathe new life into them. Just as the dry bones rose and became a mighty army, we too can rise from our circumstances and live with intention and purpose. Here are a few things to get you started:

1. **Identify the areas in your life where there is death and decay.** When I talk about identifying areas of "death and decay" in our lives, I'm referring to aspects of our existence that are stagnant, unhealthy, or even destructive. These can be physical, emotional, spiritual, or relational areas that are no longer serving us and may, in fact, be holding us back from living fully and purposefully. This could manifest in different forms such as experiencing depression, anxiety, relationships that have ended, or even dreams you have abandoned because life got in the way. Just as Ezekiel walked through the valley of dry bones, facing the reality of the desolation before him, we too must confront the broken and lifeless parts of our lives.

Denial will only prolong the suffering, but acknowledging these areas with honesty allows you to begin the healing process by inviting God into your situation. Let's explore how to identify these areas:

- *Emotional Stagnation:* Reflect on your emotional state. Are there unresolved feelings of anger, sadness, or resentment that you've been carrying for too long? Emotional stagnation can manifest as chronic bitterness, depression, or a lack of joy and enthusiasm for life. Admitting that things aren't perfect and some parts of your life feel lifeless is the first step toward healing. God doesn't need perfection from you—He needs honesty.

- *Toxic Relationships:* We've discussed relationships extensively throughout this book because they play a crucial role in shaping how we live our lives. Examine your relationships with others. Are there connections that consistently drain your energy, lower your self-esteem, or cause you stress? Relationships that are toxic or one-sided can cause decay in your personal life. It might be time to set boundaries or distance yourself from people who do not contribute positively to your growth.

- *Physical Neglect:* Consider how you treat your body. Are you neglecting your physical health through poor diet, lack of exercise, or harmful habits like overeating, smoking, or excessive drinking? Physical neglect can lead to a decline in your overall well-being, manifesting as chronic illnesses or low energy levels.

- *Spiritual Disconnection:* Take a moment to evaluate your spiritual life. Are you feeling disconnected from your faith, your sense of purpose, or meaning? Spiritual decay might manifest as a lack of direction, feelings of hopelessness, or a sense of disconnection from God. This can be a challenging area to acknowledge because it's often seen as unpopular or taboo to admit. However, many people experience spiritual disconnection but choose to hide it or pretend otherwise. I know I have at varying times throughout my life. Remember Ezekiel's words: "Lord, only you know." It's OK to admit that you are in a spiritually barren place. While God is the one who breathes life into these dry areas, it's your responsibility to recognize them and bring them to Him.

- *Professional and Creative Burnout:* Look at your professional and creative endeavors. Are you feeling unfulfilled, uninspired, or stuck in your career? Professional burnout or creative blockages can lead to a sense of decay in your work life. It's crucial to find ways to rekindle your passion or perhaps even pivot to something that aligns more closely with your purpose.

- *Habits and Routines:* Analyze your daily habits and routines. Are there patterns of behavior that are no longer serving you, such as procrastination, overindulgence, or negative thinking? These habits can contribute to a sense of decay, preventing you from moving forward and reaching your goals. Make a plan to address these behaviors and stick with it.

- *Environmental Factors:* Take a moment to reflect on your physical environment. Are you living or working in a space that feels cluttered, chaotic, or uninspiring? Think about your desk—what does it look like right now? I ask this as I stare at the stacks of papers on mine. I've noticed that I automatically feel overwhelmed when I work at my desk due to the clutter. What about your closet? I don't know about you, but when my closet is tidy and organized, it feels like my entire world is less chaotic. It's important to examine your spaces, especially the ones you spend the most time in. Your environment can have a profound impact on your mental and emotional well-being, and if it's not conducive to your growth, it can contribute to a sense of stagnation or decay.

2. Ask God for wisdom and direction in addressing these areas.

In the story of Ezekiel, God didn't just *show* him the dry bones and leave him to figure out what to do next. Instead, God provided specific instructions to *speak* life into the bones. God is ready to guide you on how to resurrect the barren and decayed areas of your life. Simply ask Him for clarity and direction on how to approach the issues you're facing. So many of us still struggle with prayer. We think we need to say all the right things and only then will God give us a response. No, Matthew 7:7 instructs us to simply ask and we will receive. Also James 1:5 tells us, "If any of you lacks wisdom, you should ask God, who gives generously to all without finding fault, and it will be given to you." This means we can ask the Lord for wisdom to understand what actions or steps we need to take to address these decaying areas of our lives. Remember, when we trust the Lord, we should not rely on our own limited human understanding (Proverbs 3:5–6). When we ask God for wisdom, we have to be vulnerable and trust that only He knows, and only He can empower us to speak life into those areas.

3. ***Listen and follow God's directions.*** After seeking God's wisdom, the next step is to listen and act on His directions. When God instructed Ezekiel to prophesy to the bones, he didn't hesitate—he obeyed. We too must be willing to act on the instructions God gives us without hesitation, even if it doesn't make sense to us. This may involve making changes in your life, letting go of certain habits or relationships, or stepping out in faith into something new. Listening to God requires patience, discernment, and courage. It's not always easy to follow His lead, especially when His instructions challenge our comfort zones or defy our understanding. However, as we obey, we open the door for God's power to work in our lives. Now, this may not happen overnight, but just as the dry bones gradually came

together and were filled with breath, so too will you begin to see life returning to the areas that were once dead. Trust in the process, remain steadfast in your faith, and know that with God, all things are possible.

Despite your past or present circumstances, remember that God can breathe life into your situation. You can reclaim your life and live with intention, knowing that God can bring forth new life and hope in even the most desolate places. No matter how lifeless your situation may seem, God can breathe life into it. You can live again!

Start Now

Making the decision to live is an exhilarating adventure filled with unknown possibilities and opportunities. I encourage you to envision the life you desire and take intentional steps toward making it a reality. Remember what I said earlier, it's a step-by-step process. You might wake up tomorrow with the intent to live fully and by the time you're ready for bed you realize that the day didn't go quite as you imagined. That's OK. Wake up the next day with the same intentionality and action. Gradually you will see your life mimicking that of the one you dreamed of.

Now, you will have to step out of your comfort zone, embrace uncertainty, and be relentless in your pursuit to live intentionally. But I promise you it will be worth it. Life will move from feeling meaningless to invigorating. You will truly be able to celebrate each new day and count it as a blessing and not a burden. You will begin to feel like you are truly living. And when that happens, hopefully, you will remember this moment and thank God you made the decision to start living.

Pause, Consider, Take Action

1. Have you ever taken a moment to define what living authentically means to you? How do you envision your own journey of living life to its fullest potential?

2. Imagine a life where money, access, and resources are not barriers. How would you choose to live? Before you rush to answer, allow me to challenge you to delve deeper than your initial thoughts. Look beyond the superficial aspects and envision how you truly want to live. I'm talking about fully embracing and enjoying life in every sense of the word.

3. In your ideal world, what would your daily routine look like? How would you spend your time? Who would you surround yourself with? Take a moment to visualize the details of your dream life, from the moment you wake up to the last thoughts before drifting off to sleep. Would you pursue passions that have long been neglected? Travel to destinations you've only dreamed of? Dive into projects that ignite your soul? The possibilities are endless when limitations are removed. So, dare to dream big and explore the depths of your desires.

4. What obstacles stand in the way of living this ideal life? Are there limiting beliefs, fears, or socictal expectations holding you back? How can you overcome these barriers and step into your fullest potential?

____

____

____

____

CHAPTER 7

Love on Top

In 2011, Beyonce released her fourth studio album titled *4*, which included the single "Love on Top." Something about the song's title has always stuck with me. I've facilitated workshops and centered speeches all around this title. The title, not necessarily the song, has been an inspiration and reminder in my life. This is why, I decided to title this chapter, "Love on Top."

In our journey toward living a purpose-filled life, it's easy to get caught up in the hustle and bustle of daily responsibilities, ambitions, and the pursuit of success. Yet, amid the chaos and the drive to achieve, there's one foundational element that should guide every action and decision: love. I believe, to truly live purposefully and embrace life fully, love must be at the forefront of all our actions, influencing every choice and interaction. Love must be on top.

The Power of Love

Love is more than a feeling; it's a transformative force that shapes our lives and the world around us. In 1 Corinthians 13:4–7, we find a beautiful and profound description of love:

"Love is patient, love is kind. It does not envy, it does not boast, it is not proud. It does not dishonor others, it is not self-seeking, it is not easily angered, it keeps no record of wrongs. Love does not delight in evil but rejoices with the truth. It always protects, always trusts, always hopes, always perseveres."

Love is a series of deliberate actions and attitudes that can transform our lives. When love is at the center of our lives, it guides how we interact with others, make decisions, and pursue our goals. Love requires intentionality. It's a conscious choice we make every day to show up with love at the center of our thoughts, words, and actions. This decision isn't always easy. It requires intention, effort, and more often than not, a willingness to push through trauma, past hurts, and disappointment. Love, in its purest form, is an expression of acceptance, understanding, and compassion—both for ourselves and for others. When we embrace love, we open our hearts to the beauty and potential within and around us.

Self-Love: The Foundation for All Relationships

The Bible instructs us to "Love your neighbor as yourself" (Mark 12:31). Yet, many find this challenging because they struggle with self-love. How can you truly love your neighbor as yourself if you don't even love yourself? Notice that the command isn't conditional; it doesn't say to love your neighbor if you love yourself, or to love your neighbor like you would love yourself. It says, "Love your neighbor as yourself." Because given that we are made in the image and likeness of God, loving yourself should be natural.

However, many people struggle to love themselves, often due to feelings of unworthiness, past mistakes, or societal pressures that make them feel inadequate. They carry burdens of self-doubt, shame, and insecurity, which hinder their ability to see themselves through God's eyes as worthy, valuable, and loved. Despite this command, they believe that loving themselves is somehow selfish or undeserved.

In recent years, self-love has become a popular topic in self-help books and motivational speeches, but what does it truly mean? How can we incorporate it into our daily lives?

First, note that self-love is not about arrogance, self-indulgence, or being self-centered. Instead, it's about recognizing your own worth, your value, and treating yourself with kindness and respect. It involves honoring your needs and desires in a balanced way, accepting who you are while still striving for growth and improvement. Self-love is a compassionate acknowledgment of your strengths and flaws, and it forms the bedrock for healthy relationships with others.

Practicing self-love begins with self-awareness. This means taking an honest look at yourself—celebrating your achievements and recognizing your worth, while also acknowledging your weaknesses without letting them define you. Everyone has made mistakes or has things they wish were different, but these do not make you any less deserving of love.

Remember, perfection is reserved for God alone. Let go of the notion that you must meet certain standards to be worthy of love. You are enough just as you are. Embracing self-love means accepting all parts of yourself: the good, the bad, and the imperfect. This doesn't mean you shouldn't strive to be the best version of yourself; rather, it means you should do so with compassion, not self-criticism. Accept that your past experiences do not define your present or your future. Treat yourself with the same kindness and understanding you would extend to a friend. Isn't it interesting how we can advise a friend or colleague to take it easy on themselves, yet we are extremely hard on ourselves?

To fully embrace this command, you must believe in what God says about you rather than relying on your own insecurities. Loving yourself means nurturing your well-being, trusting in your worth, protecting your peace and not allowing anything other than the words of your Creator to dominate your self-view. When you embrace self-love, you lay a strong foundation that extends outward, allowing you to love others more deeply and authentically.

The Outflow: Love That Transforms

Once we build a strong foundation of self-love, that love naturally flows outward, impacting every facet of our lives. This outflow of love is not just a concept—it's the practical way we connect with and uplift those around us. It has the power to transform our relationships, work environments, and even how we handle adversity.

Jesus exemplified this when He said in John 13:34: *"A new command I give you: Love one another. As I have loved you, so you must love one another."*

His life and teachings demonstrate that purpose is fulfilled through acts of love. Love motivates us to act with integrity, serve others selflessly, and live authentically.

In our relationships, whether with family, friends, or colleagues, love should be the foundation. This means showing kindness, patience, and understanding, even when it's challenging. When we approach relationships with love, we foster deeper connections and create a supportive community that enhances our journey toward purpose. Think about what would happen if you approached every interaction with empathy and warmth. It would strengthen the bonds of those you interact with and create a supportive and thriving environment.

At work, love can transform how we approach our professional lives. Leading with compassion, striving to make a positive impact, and using our skills to serve others can make our work more meaningful and fulfilling. I always refer to the work that I do as service because love has the power to change a task or job to an act of service. When love drives our professional endeavors, it turns tasks into contributions. Now, our work becomes a platform not just for achievement but for making a difference in the lives of others.

Even in adversity, love can serve as a guiding light. Challenges and hardships are inevitable, but how we choose to respond makes all the difference. It's natural to feel frustration, anger, or impatience when faced with difficulties. However, it takes intentional reflection and a pause to reframe the situation. By choosing to approach challenges with love instead of frustration, we navigate tough times with greater grace and resilience. Love empowers us to hold on to hope and persevere, transforming obstacles into opportunities for new perspectives, deeper understanding, and ultimately, self-growth.

Practical Steps to Place Love on Top

1. ***Start Each Day with Intention:*** Each morning, set a simple intention to lead with love throughout the day. Ask yourself how you can infuse kindness, empathy, and understanding into your interactions and tasks—whether it's offering a smile to a stranger or a supportive word to a friend. Personally, I love giving compliments. Whenever I interact with people, even for a brief

moment, I find something to compliment them on. Sometimes it's the most random thing, but it often brings a smile to their face. In situations where someone has pre-judged me before we meet, I've found that by intentionally complimenting them, they tend to let their guard down or reconsider their initial impression of me. A little intention goes a long way.

2. ***Practice Active Listening:*** When engaging in conversation, truly listen to what the other person is saying. We live in a society of self-proclaimed multitaskers, but the reality is that most of us aren't as good at it as we think. Active listening is one thing that cannot be multitasked. Give the person your full attention and respond with empathy, understanding and sharing their feelings by putting yourself in their situation. This approach shows that you value their thoughts and emotions, helping to build deeper and more meaningful connections.

3. ***Engage in Acts of Kindness:*** Small, thoughtful gestures can make a big difference. It might be as simple as holding the door open for someone. Don't just offer help, give it. I've noticed that many people offer to help but secretly hope the other person doesn't take them up on it. Some things don't require an offer; you can just act. For example, if you see a colleague coming from the mailroom with a handful of packages, don't just ask if they need help, grab a package or two and walk them to their desk. For those of us who find it hard to ask for help, even when the boxes are stacked so high we can't see

ahead, this kind of gesture goes a long way. Another gesture I love is writing handwritten notes. I stock up on cards from the dollar store and keep them around for whenever I see an opportunity to leave a kind message. Sometimes it's just a sticky note. If I'm working virtually, I send a short email or Slack message with a thoughtful word. Be creative, but most importantly, be thoughtful.

4. ***Reflect on Your Actions:*** Take time to regularly reflect on how love is guiding your decisions and actions. Ask yourself if there are moments where love could have been more present. If you find there are, don't be too hard on yourself. Instead, consider whether there's an opportunity for a do-over or an acknowledgment and apology, if necessary. Also, think about how you can handle similar situations better in the future. Always be willing to adjust your approach to ensure that love remains a central part of your daily life.

5. ***Seek Support:*** Your circle matters. Surround yourself with people who inspire and support your journey toward a love-centered life. If the people closest to you are consistently negative, they can hinder your efforts. You don't have to "unfriend" them, but as a friend once told me, you should rearrange where they sit on your bus. Those closest to you should be a source of support and a driving force toward your positive growth. Their encouragement and positive influence can help keep you focused on your purpose and remind you to place love at the heart of everything you do.

By incorporating these steps into your daily routine, you make love an active and integral part of your life. You'll also be making a conscious effort to bring warmth and care to every situation, which not only enriches your own life but also positively impacts those around you. Outflow!

Don't Forget Gratitude

Give thanks in all circumstances; for this is God's will for you in Christ Jesus. (1 Thessalonians 5:18)

I truly believe that love and gratitude are deeply interconnected, forming the foundation of a fulfilling and empowered life. Gratitude, is the practice of recognizing and appreciating the positive aspects of our lives, no matter how small. It shifts our focus from what we lack to what we have, fostering a mindset of abundance and contentment. When we cultivate gratitude, we begin to see the world through a lens of appreciation, which naturally deepens our capacity to love.

I've come to learn this firsthand. After years of processing on my own, trying to be more consciously self-aware, and trying not to get stuck in the past or present without losing my mind, I finally decided it was time to see a therapist. The talks with my girlfriends were not cutting it. I kept finding myself sharing the wheel with the cute little hamster I saw at Pet Smart. I was mentally, physically, financially, and emotionally exhausted. If there was a category where exhaustion was possible, I was exhausted in that category too. I found a therapist and started unpacking thirty-seven years of trauma, pain, sorrow, victory and defeat, joy and success. My therapist, a statuesque African American woman in her seventies listened and probed. We met weekly over a period of time. One particular day while I was sharing a negative occurrence from the previous week, my therapist said to me, "Tanna, I want you to remember gratitude."

I was taken aback by her words as I have always thought of myself as a grateful person. I had been through a lot in my life and was clear to thank and praise God for bringing me this far. Yet, for a period, in every session, my therapist would say, "Let's not forget gratitude." What my therapist was getting at was teaching me to get in the habit of recognizing the good even in the bad. And being grateful for the smallest of things because they help to shape our mindset and the way we interpret life. We often find it easy to focus on our problems and challenges, but it can be much harder to recognize and appreciate the small blessings we tend to overlook.

Living a grateful life unlocks a different kind of joy in our lives. Have you ever met a person who seems so unbelievably positive that you wonder if they've ever had a bad day in their lives? If you sat down with such a person and asked about their past, you'd probably learn that they have survived profound trauma. But how can they be so happy then? Well, gratefulness changes your perspective. It allows you to focus on your blessings rather than your burdens.

The connection between love and gratitude is powerful. When we practice gratitude, we nurture a sense of well-being and joy that fuels our ability to love more fully and authentically. And, when we approach life with love, we naturally become more grateful for the people, experiences, and opportunities that come our way. We can face challenges with grace, we can support and uplift each other, and find peace and fulfillment within ourselves. By intertwining love and gratitude in our daily lives, we create a ripple effect that not only transforms us but also inspires those around us.

Love Is an Action Word

Love has the incredible power to heal, inspire, and elevate us beyond our limitations. True love, whether for ourselves, others, or for life itself, is something we must always prioritize. It's not just an ideal but a practice that shapes every moment of our lives. Love should be the compass that guides you, the light that illuminates your path, and the force that propels you toward a life of purpose and fulfillment. Make love your default in every decision you make. When faced with challenges, pause and choose love over frustration. When relationships test your patience, let love guide your responses.

So, as you continue on your journey, ask yourself: How can I put love on top today? How can I let love guide my decisions, interactions, and life in general? When love is on top, you're not only creating a life that reflects the very best of who God created you to be but also making the world a better place in the process. Remember, love is an action word, and it's up to you to put it into action every single day. Embrace love on top and watch as it transforms you and the world around you.

Pause, Consider, Take Action

1. How do you define love in your life?

____

____

____

____

2. In what areas of your life do you find it difficult to put love on top?

____

____

____

3. How do you currently practice self-love? Are there areas where you struggle to show love to yourself? What might be holding you back?

4. Reflect on the biblical instruction to "Love your neighbor as yourself." How does your level of self-love affect your ability to love others? How can you nurture self-love in a healthy way?

5. Reflect on a time when gratitude helped you see the good in a difficult situation. How did this shift in perspective affect your emotional well-being and your ability to love?

6. Think about your daily routine. How can you incorporate moments of gratitude to enhance your ability to love others and yourself more deeply?

CHAPTER 8

Believe Bigger

Now to Him who is able to do exceedingly abundantly above all that we ask or think, according to the power that works in us (Ephesians 3:20)

Oh, the places we've been in this book. What a journey! As I reviewed the chapters and began writing the concluding one, I realized that something was missing. It wasn't included in the original concept or outline of the book. In fact, it came from an Advent sermon I preached in December 2022. However, it didn't start resonating with me until December 2023 and continues to do so now.

You see, in this season of my life, I am reminded that God's ability far surpasses my own understanding, desires, imagination, and prayers. I am relearning that God is not just capable of meeting needs, but He can go beyond our wildest expectations.

No matter how big you think your ideas are, no matter how big you think your prayer requests are, no matter how big you think your dreams are, God is bigger and can do bigger. So before I wrap this up I want to encourage you—implore you—to believe bigger.

Expand Your Vision

There was a small Christmas tree that I had for years, about four or five, a tiny tree that I bought on sale for maybe thirty dollars. If you know me, you know how much I love Christmas and how decorating brings me joy. But two years ago, I felt it was time for a change. I wanted to upgrade to the tree of my dreams. So, at the end of last Christmas season, I decided to donate my little tree and make room for the new tree.

That year, I took the plunge and ordered a new tree online. I had a vision in my mind of the size and look I wanted. When the tree arrived, I was excited to set it up. As I started putting it together, I thought, "This is nice. This is exactly what I wanted." But as the tree took shape, I realized that the tree was huge, so huge that it touched the ceiling.

Caden came downstairs, looked at the tree, and said, "Mommy, I think you overdid it." And honestly, I agreed. I stood there, contemplating my options. Should I take the tree down, pack it up, and return it for something smaller? Or should I go ahead and decorate it, even though it would require a lot more ornaments and a ladder to reach the top?

After some thought, I decided to decorate the tree. I had to go out and buy more decorations, but I went for it. A few hours later the tree was fully decorated. When Caden came back downstairs, he stared at the tree with a puzzled look on his face. I asked, "Caden, what's the matter? Don't you like the tree?"

He responded, still with a puzzled look, "Mommy, I like the tree." I pressed some more knowing there was something on his mind. "Then what's the matter?" He paused and responded, "Mommy, I just figured it out. The problem isn't that the tree is too big. The problem is that the house is too small."

That moment hit me like a ton of bricks. Caden gave me a new way to look at the situation and I also got a powerful realization: Sometimes, our dreams aren't too big, our vision of what's possible is just too small. And listen, just because you put a big Christmas tree in a small house doesn't mean you can't decorate it while you believe and look for a bigger house.

Stretch Your Faith

Faith is like a muscle—it grows stronger when you use it, but real growth requires stretching beyond what's comfortable. As women navigating both personal and professional challenges, it's easy to rely on what's familiar, what feels safe. Staying in our comfort zone might feel safe, but it's also where dreams go to die. When we limit ourselves to what we know, we miss out on the opportunities that require faith, the kind of faith that propels us into new territories and unlocks new potential.

True transformation comes when we dare to stretch our faith, believing that God's plans for us are far greater than anything we can imagine. To "stretch your faith" is to open yourself up to the limitless possibilities God has for you, even when those possibilities seem beyond your reach. It's stepping out on faith not because you can see the whole path, but because you believe God will light the way as you move forward.

In the Bible, we see numerous examples of individuals who stretched their faith and experienced profound and transformative outcomes. *Sarah* initially laughed at the promise of bearing a child due to her old age (Genesis 18:12). Despite her doubts, God's promise was fulfilled with the birth of Isaac (Genesis 21:1–2), reminding us that God's plans can exceed human understanding and capabilities. The story of *Esther* is another powerful example. She risked her life by approaching the king to save her people, which was a bold and dangerous move (Esther 4:16). Her faith and courage led to the deliverance of the Jews and solidified her legacy as a significant figure in biblical history.

Stretching your faith isn't about testing God, it's about trusting that God is bigger than any challenge you face. It's about believing that God can do more than you ever thought possible.

Here are some ways you can begin to exercise that faith muscle and stretch your faith:

- ***Set Bold Goals:*** One of the most effective ways to stretch your faith and empower yourself is by setting bold goals that you know will require God's intervention. While it's important to set achievable goals, don't be afraid to add goals that challenge you to rely on God's power and wisdom. When I first began setting goals for this book, they were all very safe and seemingly attainable. If a goal felt too ambitious, I would reframe it or extend the deadline to ensure it was within reach. But I realized that playing it safe wasn't beneficial for me, and honestly, it wasn't much fun either. I decided to challenge myself to dream bigger, and let me tell you, it scared me. However, throughout this process, I've seen God work in ways I never imagined. It's been incredibly exciting to see things come together, all because I dared to set bold goals. I encourage you to do the same.

- ***Take Faith-Fueled Risks:*** Whether it's launching a new business, speaking out on an issue, or making a life-changing decision, taking risks is essential to stretching your faith. These are the moments that redefine your limits and open doors to new possibilities. The parable of the talents in Matthew 25:14–30 teaches us the importance of taking risks with what God has entrusted to us. The servant who buried his talent out of fear missed out on the opportunity to multiply it. In contrast, the servants who took risks were rewarded.

Taking faith-fueled risks doesn't mean acting recklessly; it means stepping out in obedience to God's leading, even when the path isn't clear. It's trusting that God is with you, guiding your steps and providing for your needs. Proverbs 3:5–6 encourages us to "trust in the Lord with all your heart and lean not on your own understanding; in all your ways submit to Him, and He will make your paths straight." This trust is the foundation of taking risks that stretch our faith.

You can probably come up with a hundred reasons why you shouldn't take a faith-fueled risk, but I guarantee you, if you switch your perspective, you can come up with a hundred more as to why you can. The hardest part of this step is getting started. Many people often get stuck in the idea and never take the risk.

- ***Pray Audacious Prayers:*** Pray prayers that reflect the greatness of our God. Don't just pray for what's easy or expected, ask God for the extraordinary, the miraculous, the impossible. Our prayers should be bold, not because we are worthy, but because God is able. I once heard Priscilla Shirer say that she ends her prayers with the following words: "Lord, please do this ... or do something better!"

Audacious prayers are not about demanding from God but about aligning our desires with His will and trusting Him for the outcome. Ephesians 3:20 (NKJV) assures us that God is able to do "exceedingly abundantly above all that we ask or think, according to the power that works in us." When we pray audaciously, we tap into that power, inviting God to move in ways that surpass our understanding.

- ***Celebrate Past Victories:*** Reflect on the times when God came through in ways you didn't expect. Let those victories remind you that if He did it before, He can do it again. Use your past as fuel to stretch your faith even further. Your past victories are a testament to God's faithfulness. When you're facing a new challenge, look back at how God has delivered you before. Psalm 77:11–12 encourages us to "remember the deeds of the Lord" and "meditate on all His works and consider all His mighty deeds." By celebrating what God has done for us in the past, we build our confidence in God's ability to do it again, which makes it a little easier to believe bigger.

- ***Embracing Discomfort:*** Discomfort is often the birthplace of growth. When you feel uneasy or uncertain, remember that these feelings are signs that you're on the verge of something greater. Stretching your faith means embracing this discomfort and trusting that God is leading you to a place of greater purpose and power. I remember being seventeen and getting ready to preach my first sermon. I was so nervous, and I had that uncomfortable feeling in the pit of my stomach that always shows up when I'm about to do something big. Just a few moments before I was set to speak, my youth pastor came over to me. Without me even saying a word about how I was feeling, he said, "You know that uncomfortable feeling in the pit of your stomach that you're experiencing right now? That means you have something." His words instantly changed my perspective. From that day on, I began to lean into the discomfort before every major event in my life, because it reminded me that I have something valuable to share.

Discomfort is a necessary part of the growth process. It's in these moments of stretching that our character is refined, and our faith is strengthened. Remember the story I shared about my giant Christmas tree that wouldn't fit in my living room? I was so accustomed to my tiny tree fitting perfectly in my small home. But when I finally got a bigger tree, it was a revelation. Through Caden, I realized that I needed to place my trust in God for a bigger home. The discomfort and even the embarrassment of having such a large tree that didn't fit stretched my faith and helped me believe in the possibility of a larger space. Embrace the discomfort and know that God is at work. One of my favorite songs, "Waymaker," has a line that I remind myself of often: "Even when I don't see it, you're working. Even when I can't feel it, you're working. You never stop, you never stop working." Don't let the discomfort tell you otherwise.

- **_Look Around You:_** One of my favorite things to do is watch documentaries and movies about real-life individuals who dared to dream, defy the odds, or take risks. These stories fuel my faith and inspire me. I encourage you to look at women who have stretched their faith and witnessed God work in miraculous ways. Whether it's a story of overcoming personal hardships, breaking through professional barriers, or experiencing a miracle, these testimonies are powerful reminders of what can happen when we dare to believe bigger.

As you stretch your faith, you'll discover that the limits you once believed in no longer hold. God's power will transform your life and the lives of those around you in ways you never imagined. Embrace the stretch and watch as God exceeds your expectations.

Trust God Every Step of the Way

Have you ever noticed how our faith is often sparked by taking that initial step forward, but not necessarily by continuing to move forward? We take a leap of faith, but when the path becomes uncomfortable or unfamiliar, we tend to retreat to what's familiar, seeking comfort in what we know instead of trusting God to lead us through the unknown.

Consider the story of Lot in Genesis 19:17–22. God sent angels to rescue Lot and his family from the impending destruction of their city. The instructions were clear: "Flee for your lives! Don't look back, and don't stop anywhere in the plain! Flee to the mountains or you will be swept away!"

But instead of trusting God's direction and heading to the mountains as he was told, Lot hesitated. He pleaded, "Please, my lords, let me flee to this small town instead. It's near enough, and I'll be safe there." Lot chose the comfort of familiarity over the unknown of the mountains, despite God's clear instructions. He feared the mountains, convinced that he wouldn't survive the journey. But here's the thing: God had already held back the destruction to ensure that Lot and his family made it out of the city. If God could do that, surely He could also ensure Lot's safety in the mountains.

This story made me wonder: How many of us are living lives we've chosen for ourselves rather than the lives God has planned for us? How many of us are settling for a comfortable life when God is calling us to something far greater? We might be living good lives, achieving the goals we set for ourselves, but are you, as Oprah Winfrey puts it, "Living inside God's dream" for you?

Lot tried to make sense of God's instructions by choosing the small town over the mountains, but in doing so, he missed out on the greater blessings that could have awaited him in the mountains. So many of us do the same thing. We try to rationalize God's instructions, attempting to fit His plans into our understanding, and in the process, we miss out on the blessings God has for us. We're so focused on making sense of the future that we overlook what God is doing right now.

I urge you not to limit God to your own ideas of success or what feels comfortable. Believe bigger, not because it makes sense but because it makes faith; it's about faith, not logic. Trust that God sees far beyond what you can see. You might see only to the next corner, but God sees around the corner. You might see to the next city, but God sees all the way to the mountain. Don't settle for the small town when God is calling you to the mountain. Believe bigger!

Pause, Consider, Take Action

1. What are some bold goals or dreams you have hesitated to pursue because they seemed too big or out of reach? How might setting these goals stretch your faith and reveal God's power in your life?

2. Reflect on a time when you felt uncomfortable or uncertain but chose to embrace that discomfort. What did you learn from that experience, and how did it shape your growth and faith?

3. Think about women in your life or history who have demonstrated remarkable faith and courage. How have their stories inspired you to believe bigger or take faith-fueled risks?

4. Consider your current situation: Are there areas where you might be settling for less because it feels safer or more comfortable? How can you challenge yourself to trust God for more and step into a greater purpose?

EPILOGUE

As We Go

I recently had coffee with my dear friend Stephanie. Yes, it's the same Stephanie I told you about earlier, the one I walked around New York City with in four-inch stilettos for an entire summer. We caught up on our lives, sharing both our uncertainties and our hopes for the future. During our conversation, Stephanie said something that became a refrain for our time together and an ongoing mantra between us: "As we go."

Stephanie reminded me of a powerful truth from the Bible: Sometimes, the change and healing we seek don't come all at once. Instead, they unfold as we take steps forward, even when the path is unclear. In the Bible, we see several stories where people didn't receive immediate results but experienced transformation as they moved forward in faith.

Take the ten lepers in Luke 17:14: "When he saw them, he said, 'Go, show yourselves to the priests.' And as they went, they were cleansed." Their healing happened as they took those first steps.

Or consider the official in John 4:50: "'Go,' Jesus replied, 'your son will live.' The man took Jesus at his word and departed. While he was still on the way, his servants met him with the news that his boy was living." His son's healing came as he moved forward in belief.

Then there's Naaman in 2 Kings 5:14: "So he went down and dipped himself in the Jordan seven times, as the man of God had told him, and his flesh was restored and became clean like that of a young boy." Naaman's healing wasn't immediate; it came as he followed through with the instructions.

We often think we need everything to fall perfectly into place before we take the next step, or that we have to wait for all the answers before beginning something new. But sometimes, clarity and change come not before or after we act, but as we act. God doesn't always work in a straight line. Life isn't always going to make sense or go according to plan. But God isn't looking for our understanding, God is looking for our faith.

Right now, I'm in one of those seasons where not much makes sense. I have so many decisions before me, and there's a lot of uncertainty about what lies ahead. The only thing that felt certain was finishing this book. I questioned what finishing it would add to my life and if it was worth it. But then I remembered that part of our work in living, loving, and leading is embracing those moments of uncertainty and moving forward, even when we don't have all the answers. So I pressed forward, even when I didn't feel like it, and with each step came more clarity and understanding. Sometimes, simply completing something we've set out to do becomes a beacon of clarity. Remember, two things can be true at once. We can feel uncertain and still choose to act.

Throughout these chapters, I've encouraged, challenged, and inspired you with the hope that it will lead you to live a purpose-filled life. But I know that even with hope and intentionality, you might still be facing turmoil, hurt, or pain. It's easy to doubt whether your circumstances can change or whether you even deserve a fulfilling life because of past choices. To you, dear reader, I echo Stephanie's words to me: "It's as we go."

> As we dream,
> As we walk,
> As we declare,
> As we speak,
> As we move forward,
> As we build,
> As we begin,
> As we launch—
> It's as we go!

It's about finding purpose even when the path isn't clear and trusting that every step you take has meaning, even if the impact isn't immediately visible.

I titled this book ***Her Work, Live Love Lead: A Woman's Guide to Living on Purpose*** with the intention of guiding you toward living a purposeful life, loving deeply, and leading with intention. Even though I didn't explicitly focus on leadership as much as the other themes, know this: When you are intentional about living out these principles, you are already leading. You lead by example, by courage, and by your commitment to a life well lived.

As we close our time together, remember this: Even when life feels chaotic and decisions seem overwhelming, keep moving forward with intention. Embrace the work of living with purpose, loving deeply, and leading with example. It's in these practices that we often find our way through the confusion and come out stronger on the other side.

We're in this together. Throughout the book, I've used the term "we" because I want you to know that you're not alone. I'm not an expert, just a facilitator on this journey, learning and growing as I go. My prayer is that as you go, you will find strength, purpose, and unspeakable joy.

You've got this, and God's got you.

Appendix

Jeremiah 29:11 New International Version

"For I know the plans I have for you," declares the Lord, "plans to prosper you and not to harm you, plans to give you hope and a future."

Isaiah 43:19 New Revised Standard Version

"I am about to do a new thing; now it springs forth; do you not perceive it? I will make a way in the wilderness and rivers in the desert."

2 Corinthians 10:3–5 New Revised Standard Version

Indeed, we live as humans but do not wage war according to human standards, for the weapons of our warfare are not merely human, but they have divine power to destroy strongholds. We destroy arguments and every proud obstacle raised up against the knowledge of God, and we take every thought captive to obey Christ.

Matthew 7:7 New International Version

Ask and it will be given to you; seek and you will find; knock and the door will be opened to you.

James 1:5 New International Version

If any of you lacks wisdom, you should ask God, who gives generously to all without finding fault, and it will be given to you.

Proverbs 3:5–6 New International Version

Trust in the Lord with all your heart and lean not on your own understanding; in all your ways submit to him, and he will make your paths straight.

1 Corinthians 13:4–7 New International Version

Love is patient, love is kind. It does not envy, it does not boast, it is not proud. It does not dishonor others, it is not self-seeking, it is not easily angered, it keeps no record of wrongs. Love does not delight in evil but rejoices with the truth. It always protects, always trusts, always hopes, always perseveres.

Mark 12:31 New International Version

"The second is this: 'Love your neighbor as yourself.' There is no commandment greater than these."

John 13:34 New International Version

"A new command I give you: Love one another. As I have loved you, so you must love one another."

1 Thessalonians 5:18 New International Version

Give thanks in all circumstances; for this is God's will for you in Christ Jesus.

Psalm 77:11–12 New International Version

I will remember the deeds of the Lord; yes, I will remember your miracles of long ago. I will consider all your works and meditate on all your mighty deeds.

Ephesians 3:20–21 New King James Version

Now to Him who is able to do exceedingly abundantly above all that we ask or think, according to the power that works in us, to Him be glory in the church by Christ Jesus to all generations, forever and ever. Amen.

Reflections for the Journey

Without awareness and intentionality, we are prone to linger in familiar territory.

The opposite of a friend is not an enemy. It's a person who no longer holds the same significance they once did.

Trust your Creator, the author and finisher of your faith, the One who holds you in the palm of His hand. Trust that, in both uncertainty and certainty, God still knows best.

Change can be scary, and not knowing what will happen next can be unsettling, but peace is priceless.

> *Change in our community is necessary and inevitable, and while it can be challenging, it also brings opportunities for growth and empowerment. Embracing change in our community can lead to the creation of deeper, more meaningful relationships and a stronger sense of community.*

If you ever make the choice to move forward in silence, ensure that you have the proper support in place to help you navigate the silence. Supports such as a trusted friend, a therapist, or a support group. **Most importantly, make a plan to remove yourself from the person and/or environment that is causing you to move in silence. Then, execute that plan. While moving in silence is a choice, it should only be temporary, it cannot be a permanent state of being.**

While it may be painful, it is important to remember that letting go of relationships that no longer serve you creates space for new, healthier connections and personal growth.

Living doesn't mean ignoring your past experiences or present reality; it means moving forward despite them.

Staying in our comfort zone might feel safe, but it's also where dreams go to die.

> *No matter how lifeless our situations may seem, God can breathe new life into them.*

Making the decision to live is an exhilarating adventure filled with unknown possibilities and opportunities. Envision the life you desire and take intentional steps toward making it a reality.

By intertwining love and gratitude in our daily lives, we create a ripple effect that not only transforms us but also inspires those around us.

Even when life feels chaotic and decisions seem overwhelming, keep moving forward with intention. Embrace the work of living with purpose, loving deeply, and leading with example. It's in these practices that we often find our way through the confusion and come out stronger on the other side.

*Sometimes, clarity and change come
not before or after we act, but as we act.*

You've got this,
and God's got you.